From the Mouth of God

Changing Life Struggles to Powerful Energy

Richard Dupuis
with
Scott Penmann

BookPartners
Wilsonville, Oregon

Other books by Richard Dupuis:
  Ancient Wisdom
  Creating Your Light Body

Cover design by Richard Ferguson
Text design by Sheryl Mehary

BookPartners, Inc.
P.O. Box 922
Wilsonville, Oregon 97070

Table of Contents

Jesus testified that man shall not live by bread alone, but by every word that proceedeth out of the mouth of God. This memorable passage signifies that man's body does not depend only on external sources of life force — distillations from breath, oxygen, sunshine, solids and liquids — but also on a direct inner source of cosmic life that enters the body through the medulla, flowing then to the subtle centers in the brain and spine. In man, the medulla is spoken of as "the mouth of God" because it is the chief opening for the divine influx of cosmic vibratory life force, the "Word" that then flows "out of the mouth of God" to the reservoir of life energy in the brain and the distributing centers in the spine.

Paramahansa Yogananda
Commentary on the Bhagavad-gita

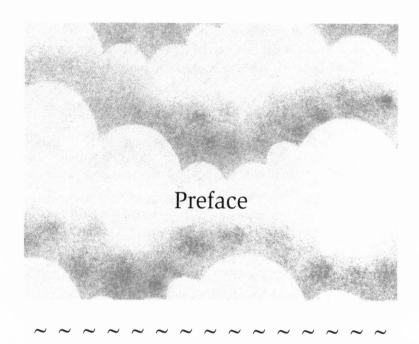

Preface

~ ~ ~ ~ ~ ~ ~ ~ ~ ~ ~ ~ ~ ~ ~

It's been said that the truth will set you free. Probably anyone who thinks about it is aware of not being too sure what "the truth" is. No matter what state a life is in, the truth has remained evasive. Discovering what the truth is for you will change the very nature of your life, raise your consciousness, and enable you to instill a new philosophy to live by.

Freedom comes from understanding yourself and knowing who you are. Freedom comes from a clear vision and understanding of the truth, and the truth is always simple. Why? If it's not kept simple, it gets lost in mental gymnastics and becomes just another concept to be filed away in the computer that is your brain. We are presenting universal principles in this book, principles that reflect truth. You may find other truths elsewhere that are every bit as important to you as these. Still, you won't get far in your attempt to survive and improve your life without integrating the basic universal principles we've written about in this book.

Working with groups and individuals, my experience as a teacher has been that many try, but few succeed, to find satisfaction and fulfillment without acknowledging these basic truths. They are universal in nature and cannot be avoided and overlooked forever. Sooner or later you will embrace them, and when you do your life will change.

Your understanding of your true nature can propel you forward at an astronomical rate. You'll gain prosperity, purpose, satisfaction, fulfillment, and anything else you're searching for if you honor these principles. You cannot live a life of joy without these principles and without them, no matter what you achieve, it will be a hollow victory. Truth is the elixir of joy and love; nothing else will bring you lasting success or happiness.

Although we'll delve into many principles, the most basic of them is that you can live your life without a connection to God — without a connection to your soul — and be completely directed by ego and personality. You may even be able to convince yourself that you are happy, but sooner or later the stress of a life in which you do not know who you really are will cause that life to fail. Health, relationships, money, one or all of these will fall away from you and you'll be left standing naked, desperately seeking the truth of your own existence.

You find love, wisdom and understanding by living in alignment with universal truths and principles. In this book they are simple, they are few in number, and they truly will set you free.

Richard Dupuis
Scott Penmann
May, 1997

1

As You Think

~ ~ ~ ~ ~ ~ ~ ~ ~ ~ ~ ~ ~ ~ ~

Dr. Albert Einstein once said that you cannot solve a problem with the same kind of thinking that created the problem. If you feel your life has gone off course and you aren't able to right it, it's because the life tools you're using are inadequate for the job at hand. In fact, those life tools probably created the problems to begin with.

In order to improve and change the content and quality of your life, you have to develop a new way of thinking, a new philosophy for life. If you don't change the way you think about yourself and the world around you, you'll be bound to repeat the same patterns, and the fabric of your life will be the same tomorrow as it is today. You may have to explore your old psychological tapes, those habitual thinking programs that have you stuck, and it will take a great deal of trust to let go of those patterns, even though they probably do not serve you anymore. In fact, they're what created the painful experiences of your life to begin with. There is no magic bullet or quick fix available, here in this book or elsewhere, but you can begin to turn away from the storms you are encountering. Whatever form this growth takes is up to you.

At one of my workshops, we were discussing what type of fundamental change is necessary to re-create one's life. A woman stood and shared that she loved change and made a habit of making changes in her life. She spoke of changing jobs or moving to another location where the energy was better for her. There is a branch of astrology that focuses on the geographical location for an individual that would create the greatest potential for success in life, and one such astrologer had recommended to her that she move. She even talked of simply rearranging the furniture in her house to create change for herself. Although all of those things might have had some benefit for her, they are mostly symbolic. I suggested that she see me for a regression session so that we could look at her subconscious thoughts and beliefs.

During our first session we discovered her belief that what she wanted in life was out of her reach. Your thoughts and beliefs are like magnets. Whatever is their focus is what they attract into your life and what appears in your experience. Life is what you think it is. Over a few sessions we released her old thinking patterns and beliefs and replaced them with positive thoughts and affirmations of her ability to achieve her desires. Immediately, her life began to change and she decided not to sell her house.

The reasons you want to change the conditions of your life can be many. You could be feeling anything from dissatisfaction and disappointment to those uneasy feelings in your gut that tell you the course you are on simply will not take you where you want to go. There are any number of books about making money and experiencing prosperity, but a successful and fulfilling life doesn't come from a handbook for making money. Nor does it suddenly fall out of the blue when you finally meet your soul mate. No amount of money, no relationship with the sexiest, most attractive person you have ever met will create a life for you that is truly gratifying.

Your thoughts can also affect your health. Disease is a symbolic response to fearful thoughts. Ron came to me to explore an odd physical problem he'd had for years: his tear ducts didn't work, and he was forced to use eye drops to lubricate his eyes. During a counseling session, I regressed him to several points where the thought came out that he would never cry again. This thought originated from an incident with his father, who had chastised Ron severely for crying. I spent a lot of time during the next two sessions trying to lead him to his own awareness of what had happened and exactly why his tear ducts had ceased to function. But he resisted my suggestion that it was a self-created emotional or psychological issue. To this day, as far as I know, Ron still uses eye drops to lubricate his eyes.

It may be difficult for you to see exactly how you are going to create a new philosophy. Again, you can't solve the problems of your life with the same kind of thinking that created the problems. You learned your current version of truth by the time you were three years old, and it became your reality. The years between then and now have been spent simply practicing what you learned then. The question you have to ask yourself is whether or not you really believe that you were taught a version of reality that will work for you today.

A species' or an individual's ability to adapt and change determines its chances for survival. The human population on earth is obviously being tested in its ability to survive. The planet is becoming overcrowded; the water, air and earth are polluted to the point that life is threatened with extinction. If we don't change something soon, we may cease to exist as a race. Ancient myths speak of civilizations that have failed to adapt — Atlantis, Lemuria, and so forth. Whether or not you believe those myths, there is little doubt that the earth is being stressed by pollution and neglect at this point in our history. Today it is up to individuals to decide what change is necessary. If you can change your thinking, and thereby your entire life, you will be widening the pathway that is the road to survival for modern mankind.

Almost everyone knows there is something missing from life, but what it is and how to remedy it is not so easy to discern. Many people have begun to search for that missing something they suspect must be hiding just around the corner. People are seeking the meaning of their lives, the nature of their existence and an understanding of their spirituality. The reason many are having trouble finding these things is because the answer is too simple. If it's so simple how come you and I have lived so many years without knowing? Because there are those who profit from your ignorance. Yes, Virginia, there are people who want to keep you dependent on them so they may keep their status and power. God has not made the truth complicated, mankind has. Jesus preached to a simple, mostly illiterate population. Do you think his message was complicated? It wasn't. It was to love God, to love yourself and to love your neighbor. His mission never would have gotten off the ground if the truths he put forth were not easily understood.

We want you to be able to change your way of thinking and create a new understanding of your reality as quickly as possible, rather than searching for two decades like we have. Changing your basic beliefs about life can be as simple or as difficult as you choose to make it. One of the things you're going to have to accept is that the larger version of reality we've been taught is inaccurate. The philosophies upon which our society has to date been built are full of holes that leave countless questions unanswered.

For example, most of us have been led to believe that God keeps secrets from us and that some things are not meant for man to know. Whether you believe there is a God or simply a higher power, it's hard to believe that the intelligence that birthed Christ, Buddha, Ghandi, and Mother Teresa would keep the truth of existence a secret from Its creations.

The greatest illusion is your knowledge of good and evil — your acceptance of polarity. The effects of this belief have caused more havoc for humankind than anything else. The knowledge of good and evil creates judgment, because if something is evil, it cannot be good. Judgment creates imbalance and polarization. When Adam and Eve ate the fruit from the Tree of Life and gained knowledge of good and evil, they fell from grace. And so have you, for the same reason. As soon as they began to believe that some of the conditions of existence were not good, there emerged in the mind of man a threat. When Adam and Eve lived in grace, they did not know fear. Up until then, Eve had no fear of the snake, they weren't ashamed to be naked, the world was full of abundance, and they had no concerns for their daily needs. But suddenly things changed when they became aware of good and evil. Fear became a way of thinking, an ungracious stance from which we all would eventually come to view our world.

Life, for many, feels like a war zone, like tiptoeing blindfolded through a minefield, just waiting for the explosion to happen. You struggle to make a living, you're at odds with family members to be understood, and you fight for acceptance or approval at work or wherever you are. No one understands you, appreciates you, or understands your pain. Of course they do not and cannot see who you are or know your pain until you yourself understand it. It is *your* judgment that the outer world can hurt you and your reaction to that perceived threat that creates pain in your life. It also spurs the most senseless behavior, blaming others for the conditions of your life.

Polarities are man-made. They exist in the mind of mankind. There are no polarities unless you believe there are. There is really only experience. As a collective and as individuals, we decide that certain behaviors are evil and that others are good. On the face of it that is true, and in this culture especially, nothing seems so ridiculous as to say there is no evil when a heinous crime occurs. However, when you judge what someone else is doing, you become polarized and fall from grace. This is why Jesus refused to stone the woman who'd been accused of adultery, but said, "He who is without sin, let him cast the first stone." No matter how hard we fight criminal behavior and how much money we spend making new laws, we cannot stop or prevent certain acts. We can only stop judging them, and thereby return to grace.

Obviously we humans haven't done very well creating a heaven on earth by using our judgment to make things right. This is largely due to our inability to hear anything other than the fear-based chatter of society. When you're able to step out of polarity and judgment, you can live in a state of grace.

We call this state of grace the neutral zone. It is that space in which your perception and judgment of good and evil do not interfere with the wisdom that is available to you. If you are not labeling everything around you as either good or evil, you open a conduit for wisdom and information to come to you from God and from your own higher nature.

The most significant polarities are the opposites of love and fear. You cannot live life successfully until you learn to walk through your fears and move beyond them. Initially, the things you fear seem awfully real when encountered and it often feels as if your fears will devour you. Of course, fear served primitive man well as a survival mechanism. Carnivores roamed the land when humans first came to earth, and fear was a useful tool to avoid becoming a tasty meal. However, today there is little threat that we will be ambushed by prowling lions. The only real danger to our survival is our own manner of thinking. If it doesn't change, we'll become our own predator.

This is one area where the advanced intellect of mankind can be very useful. When fear arises you can assess the relative danger, as well as the benefits of facing your fear. You can also learn to dissociate from your fears and choose to not make them real. This will take you quickly out of polarization. Face your fear and it will disappear. This is a very old and very true adage. Transformed by action, knowledge and understanding, fear that is faced quickly loses its ability to stop you from pursuing your goals.

A woman in her mid-twenties came to see me for counseling. Her own thinking constantly spoke to her of the futile nature of her college study. She had wanted to be an anthropologist, but her thoughts were so overwhelmingly negative that she had dropped out of school. As we explored the origin of her thoughts, we discovered that they were not her thoughts at all, but her mother's nagging thoughts and beliefs about her chosen field of endeavor. Once this was uncovered, she was quickly able to let go of those thoughts, and almost immediately started school again. She received scholarships, and subsequently secured a commission to do work for the Smithsonian Institute.

Jane was raised in a strict Christian home in which there was a lot of focus on the evils of society and the work of the Devil. Her family was very fearful and polarized. Naturally, she grew up thinking this was the way things were everywhere in the world. Jane believed that if you were not constantly vigilant, the Devil and the evil of this world would overcome you. Her thoughts were filled with fear, and she constantly attracted people of ill intent into her life who stole from her and took advantage of her. For a graduation present, Jane received a video camera. One night when she was at home watching television with her latest boyfriend, he asked her to go to the store and get something for them to eat, which she did. When she returned home the boyfriend and the video camera were gone, both never to be seen again.

Jane had been reading the chapter on beliefs in my book *Ancient Wisdom,* where I present how your beliefs create your reality. After attending one of my workshops in which I addressed how your thoughts and perceptions create your experiences, she called me and requested a personal session. She had read a number of other books that had touched on similar points. She had even run across a quote from the Bible, "As you believe it shall be done unto you."

This exposure to the material she was reading and discovering that quote had convinced her that the negative experiences in her life were coming from within herself. This was a major turning point in her life because her familial training was just the opposite. At my suggestion Jane began to meditate and spend time contemplating those areas of her life where negative patterns kept repeating. For instance, the boyfriend who'd stolen the video camera, and other male friends who often took advantage of her. She began to look for the beliefs that created the experience. When you commit to finding the truth it is always forthcoming. The awareness created by her exploration began to give her a great deal of insight into her experience.

As she began to change her thinking, her life followed suit. Within six months of Jane's revelation she received the video camera in the mail, with a note of apology from the boyfriend.

As Jane discovered, insight and awareness always create change: they are the foundation of all therapeutic processes. You can take these simple steps yourself. Take the time to meditate, to contemplate, and especially to pray for help to change. You have to change your philosophical underpinnings that are based on fear, and the idea of polarization. Keep doing what you have been doing and thinking the way you have been, and you will get what you have always gotten. To think of the difficulty and magnitude of making those changes may make you shudder. Remember how frightening it was the first time you sat in the driver's seat with those other cars hurtling toward you? Yet you realized early on that in order to experience life fully you were going to have to be in traffic, no matter how afraid you were.

Like that experience, how many times have you garnered the courage to walk through your fear, and then wondered what all the fuss was about after having reached the other side? The imagined consequences of fear are always exaggerated. As you turn inward and begin to think differently and act without becoming polarized, you will find a whole new world opening to you. It is in this new world that you will hear the voice of your soul, and connect with the spirit of God. From that comes the courage to trust your new way of thinking and to leave behind what you have held dear for so long: the road blocks to your own prosperity and sovereignty.

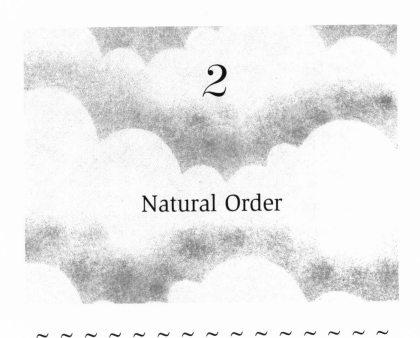

Natural Order

~ ~ ~ ~ ~ ~ ~ ~ ~ ~ ~ ~ ~ ~ ~

Theoretically, in the twentieth century with all the technology and modern conveniences we enjoy, living should be easier and more prosperous for everyone. Still, for many there is a gradual erosion of the quality of their lives. No doubt, like many people, you have an inner sense that something is changing as though the very fabric of the world you live in is changing. You're right. What you're experiencing is an energy shift. The energies that have supported the economic and religious systems of the world in the past are evolving and changing. A new paradigm is being created for humanity. You've been trained to work and compete in an era when conditions were very different from what they are today. You were taught to live and work within a paradigm that is no longer valid. The truth is that the old ways never really worked, it only seemed that way. Certainly if you look at the world today you can see that what we've created out of that old paradigm has endangered life on earth.

You grew up in a male-dominated, patriarchal society in which the theme was control. A patriarchal system is a "take-charge," rigid, and unimaginative system in which whoever fights his way to the top is the king of the hill. Leaders are respected and followed out of blind allegiance, simply because they are in authority, regardless of who they are or the types of people they are. Authority begins to assume the role of God, and will continue to do so as long as it is left unquestioned.

This patriarchal system began to break down in the sixties, but it wasn't until the eighties that the effects of this change were felt by all. Make no mistake, the paradigm your parents, your grandparents, and their grandparents operated from will not work for you in your life today. Of course it didn't really work for them either. You can see the old guard continually trying to reestablish itself. When things go wrong, how do those in charge respond? They establish more rules, laws, regulations, restrictions, safeguards and so on. This piling of controls upon controls is what has brought our society to its current state of dysfunction. We are trapped behind the doors to our homes, if we are fortunate enough to have homes. Individually, and as a whole, we are losing ground fast. Control does not work. In order to make your life work, you must stop trying to control it. But it's not easy because your ego — your personality — loves control. Controlling gives your ego a sense of power; yet in truth, to have a tight grip on anything is to smother it.

I was raised in a family where iron-fisted will and physical courage were all that mattered. You got what you wanted out of life by sheer force of will, with a little manipulation thrown in, in case force alone was not enough. In my mid-twenties I went into business for myself. For a number of years I was successful applying what I had learned as a child, which was the exact opposite of the meek inheriting the earth. In our household the meek were pushed out of the way, if not stepped on.

Back in the mid-seventies I had a large carpet cleaning company with branches all over the Midwest and on the West Coast. To increase business we turned to telephone solicitation, unusual at the time though common today. After some years in business things gradually began to go wrong. My response was to apply more control, more force of will. In the past this was always the solution, but I found that after a certain point, force and will no longer worked. My therapist at the time suggested that I give up control, sit back, and listen to what was being said by my employees, allowing them to take charge.

So I did. I called a meeting with my management staff and explained to them that I was burned out trying to control all the facets of this business and was at my wits' end, and we were losing money. Initially they suggested the usual superficial remedies: take a vacation (while we were losing money?): go fishing or golfing. But when my staff realized that I was serious and was actually willing to let go of a great deal of control, they became sincerely involved in finding solutions.

One of my employees suggested that I do what he did when a solution seemed unobtainable — ask God for an answer and meditate. Prior to that I'd never thought of meditation as a way to solve problems.

Phone solicitation was very labor intensive and costly, and we needed a way to reduce costs. One of my staff was an experienced door-to-door salesperson and he suggested we use a technique commonly used by direct salespeople: give a ten percent discount to the home owner in exchange for two referrals. As simple as it sounds, it was an incredible success.

I was astounded. Had I not given up control, we would never have had the success that we did. It was my first experience of consciously giving up control, but certainly not my last. It's not easy. Even to this day, I find that surrendering and staying out of control takes constant vigilance, because it is by no means easy to give up our childhood conditioning.

We ignore the idea that the universe is a loving, supporting place in which we are never alone. There is a divine intelligence (call it God or whatever you choose) that guides the activity of all celestial bodies. That intelligence guides our planet through its orbit around the sun, creating the seasons and the day and night. It beats your heart and spins the atoms that make up your body; it provides the divine spark for your existence. Be assured that there is a plan for your life, a plan conceived by that intelligence. This blueprint, when followed, will bring you true fulfillment and satisfaction. When it is ignored, the path that is your life becomes bumpy.

There is a natural order to life that affects everything. Any attempt to manipulate that order by any means prevents and distorts all naturally occurring consequences, which are infinitely more beneficial than anything you can fabricate with your ego's expectations. All of your successes in life, large or small — whether you know it or not — are the result of your alignment with the natural order of the universe. People have sought to live outside of the natural order, in a kind of no-man's land. But when you're living in the neutral zone and not judging the events of your life as good or bad (which always leads to an attempt to fix the bad) you will experience fulfillment. We've lost sight of this way of being to the point where few even realize the possibility that such a life exists.

So exactly who is in charge of your life? You? Your ego? Your soul? God? The truth is that there is a natural process of co-creation between you and God — that is, when you're not trying to create by edict and force of will. Living in the neutral zone is exactly the opposite of taking charge of your life. Up until this point, you've been trying in vain to take charge, haven't you? If that had worked, you wouldn't be reading this book. It's time for you to surrender the grip you hold on your reality, and to allow the natural process of co-creation to proceed.

Humans are pleasure-seeking and will avoid pain at all costs, which is, of course, an attempt at controlling the natural rhythms and cycles of life. Pain and suffering may seem like an unnatural part of your life, but these are mostly the result of perception. The loss of a business, the breakup of a relationship, these are perceived by you as incredibly painful. Yet death is half of the cycle of life. An end to things as we know them simply creates opportunity for something better in the future. As soon as you let go of your need to know exactly how you will be supported by God, you *will* be supported by God completely, and *exactly* as needed.

In the neutral zone, you suspend your need to be sure of the outcome of any situation. You can never know consciously what the outcome of your actions will be, but you can trust that every action you take is leading you to something that will enhance your life. This does not mean that by saying you believe God supports you, you will then be freed from taking any action yourself. You must act to create anything. When you are acting in accordance with the Universe's principles, every action will take you to higher ground with an economy of effort.

The intelligence of the divine mind that birthed you is inherent in your personal energies, even in the cells of your body. The intelligence of the universe is accessible from what we call the neutral zone. The neutral zone is that moment when all judgment is suspended, when you yourself are not polarized. From this space, you can easily hear the intelligence of the universe speak. Your soul understands the universal principles that apply to all forms of creation. These universal principles are very simple and few in number. Maybe you don't believe there is a divine plan for your life, or for the nations of the Earth. Maybe you feel that mankind is creating a better life for his children by taking charge of his destiny. But the ignorance and chaos seen everywhere certainly speak of something else.

When we elect new leaders in this democracy (who rarely ever lead), we choose those whom we think can gain control over whatever seems to be out of control, i.e., the economy, drugs, violence in the streets, etc. For a while it might seem to work; the economy increases, violent crimes may decrease. However, real change is always the result of growth in consciousness. Lasting change occurs in your awareness, not as the result of being smart enough to pass laws that cover every facet of a fear-ridden society. Of course, the more out of control things get, the harder society and individuals try to grasp the reigns.

Enlightened masters in the Far East can foretell the occurrence of an accident that will harm them, but they do not always attempt to avert it. These are humans totally familiar with the laws of cause and effect. They do not consider control as appropriate behavior. However, this does not mean that I recommend that if you become aware of an approaching catastrophic event in your life you do nothing to avoid it. On the other hand, being aware of a danger doesn't ensure that it, or something like it, will not happen to you in the future. In fact, it probably cannot be avoided unless you develop an understanding of why that event might occur in your life, and then act toward change.

A better future is created not by law, but by understanding and insight. Most of my adult life I was an entrepreneur. When fewer ideas and opportunities started coming to me, I stopped developing business because I felt it was due to circumstances beyond my control. I became a loner and worked jobs that relied solely on my individual effort. The whole turn of events seemed like the cruelest of circumstances. How could this happen to me, and why me? What had I done? But eventually awareness and understanding began to creep in, and with that came the realization that the true nature of the game of life being played out here on earth was in opposition to almost everything I was learning. What I have learned since then was that life doesn't have to be a struggle, that when you let go of struggle answers come naturally. Where do they come from? They come from God. Some would argue that they come from your intuition, your human nature, or even the angels, but that is just so much semantic nonsense. It is all one thing, God. You are the personification of God in the physical. God will assist you if you give him a chance. That will only happen when you are allowing him to, and not trying to control and run everything.

Control is really an aspect of fear, which puts you into a contracted, polarized state where you cannot hear God speak.

As a child I was taught that I would be rewarded for hard work and effort. My only experience was that the more effort and struggle I invested, the less they returned. This is, of course, a cultural attitude and belief, and it is absolutely false. It took me decades to discover that you're rewarded for creativity, not effort.

Our society says that God is "out there somewhere" and you can only connect with him in church or during some other sacred event. Like many social beliefs, the opposite is the real truth. You are inherently connected to God and he is always talking to you, and through you. All you really have to do is cast your desire into the wind, and through prayer your desire will come back to you. You probably remember this from the Bible: Ask and you will receive, knock and the door will open. Seek and ye shall find. Isn't this simply the way it is? It is for me.

No one wants to be in opposition to universal principles, but you've learned this behavior from your parents, so it's not easy to overcome your present way of thinking and living. Your early life is one of restriction and control. You're restricted because you don't know what is good for you, you don't know how to behave, how to stay safe. Surely, without all that control, restriction and supervision, death or other some catastrophic event would occur — or so we're conditioned to believe. As a result of this conditioning, you developed a belief in the effectiveness of control. How could you do otherwise? This belief is carried into adult life, when we *do* know how to behave and stay safe and yet that early conditioning stays with us, making us feel compelled to control all areas of our lives.

When I first met Patricia, she was in law enforcement and wanted to change the work she did, which she felt was very unsuited to her nature. She was slight of build and not very tall, yet she found herself battling drug addicts and alcoholics as part of her daily routine. What was keeping her stuck in her job and unable to change was that she'd been abused as a child. As a result, she formed a pattern of needing to control her life. As a police officer she was in control. Subconsciously, she could not release that role.

The root of control is fear. Danger lurks behind every bush, every closed door, every alley, and control is the only thing that will work, because it feels safe. The tighter you hang on to something, the less likely it is to slip out of your grasp. I love the illustration of the Chinese finger puzzle, and I can't help but wonder if the Far East inventor who came up with it had our compulsive need to control in mind. A Chinese finger puzzle is a small sleeve that fits snugly over your index fingers. When you try to remove your fingers, the sleeve only tightens, and the more you pull and struggle, the more it tightens. Only by relaxing your fingers together rather than apart — going against your instinct — will you allow the sleeve to relax and slip off your fingers.

Believing in the righteousness of fear is a belief in a false God. Fear has claimed as its domain and territory all that we are as a society. When you surrender to your fear and act to control a perceived threat, you have given up the most basic universal principle of all, trust. You create change in your life through awareness, understanding and insight, not through control. Life is created to be joyful and fulfilling. You have the right to experience your life as a movable feast, not a faithless journey of struggle and enslaving toil.

You always get more of what you put your attention on. You think that by applying more control you will get a better result. Actually you create more of what you don't want by trying to control it, and thereby create more need for more control. It becomes a never-ending cycle, as you can see in all areas of our society. What looks like control is really interference with the natural order of the universe and its innate intelligence.

The universe is forever seeking balance. When your feelings and emotions are out of balance you'll experience something that causes an emotional upheaval. This is a natural order seeking balance. Life is completely symbolic. What you experience externally is the result of your inner landscape. Even the work you do, the career you choose, will represent your inner world, as for Patricia who chose to work in law enforcement. One of the symptoms of sexual abuse is the victim's need to control. Drug and alcohol abuse are also an attempt at controlling the inner world through external interdiction. Reformed alcoholics often become control addicts. They've given up their drug addiction for yet another addiction.

Your personality, or ego, is completely invested in control. It believes control can work, and it will move heaven and earth to prove it to you, no matter the cost. Because your ego is conditioned by previous training, it always projects the past onto your present and your beliefs about the future. Of course your ego is going to do this. After all, it's how we as humans learn about the natural world: that innocent stove was hot and burned you in the past, so it's hot today, and will be tomorrow. Your ego actually thinks it's protecting you, which is why your ego will try so hard to prove to you that control can work. But in those areas where you have adopted beliefs from your early experiences that are out of sync with universal principles and reality, you will continue to repeat and reinforce those beliefs. Trying harder, struggling, and putting more effort into resolving your problems might give you temporary relief, but treating the symptoms never works. That is simply more control, which puts you at odds with a real solution.

If you accept the premise of this chapter — that control does not work, that it is actually a roadblock to fulfillment and understanding — then the next step is learning trust. Don't allow the temptation of fear to dictate your thinking. This will take continuous, ongoing monitoring of your choices, responses, and thoughts. The reward is that you will be free to become more conscious, more aware, and more in touch with that grander part of your soul and spirit that is your divine intelligence.

3

Trust and Faith

~ ~ ~ ~ ~ ~ ~ ~ ~ ~ ~ ~ ~ ~ ~

"And Jesus said unto them, 'Because of your unbelief: for verily I say unto you, If ye have faith as a grain of mustard seed, ye shall say unto this mountain, Remove hence to yonder place; and it shall remove; and nothing shall be impossible to you.'" (Matthew 17:20) With this statement, Jesus was saying that when you know without question — when you trust and have faith — the door is open for things to happen in your life that are beyond your current comprehension. Jesus spoke a simple truth, that what he did, you can also do, only more so. He was aware of the fact that he was the son of God. Did that make him special? Jesus healed the sick and brought the dead back to life. Moses parted the Red Sea. Were these miracles? Were these miracle workers different from the rest of us? The leaders of today's Christian religions would have you believe that Jesus is the only son of God, but that is not the truth. The miracles these men performed were demonstrations of complete faith which any human being of equal faith could also accomplish.

A Course in Miracles, which was also given to us by Jesus, states that there are no special souls. Every soul is unique in its self-expression, but all are created equally. There have been and are today many souls whose awareness equals Jesus's own, souls who have come to earth to prophesy, leaving behind great spiritual wisdom and knowledge. The Vedas are a Hindu tradition that preceded Jesus by at least 3,000 years. Translated, Veda means "knowledge." Whether you find your inspiration from the Vedas, the Bhagavad-gita, the Cabala, or the Bible, you will ultimately find that when you combine your trust with knowing, you become the Master.

Your soul knows truth. In fact, it knows only truth. Certainly sometime in our past we, as humans, knew the truth of our existence. Even today there are isolated groups or tribes of people who know the truth. A popular book entitled *Mutant Message Downunder,* by Marlo Morgan, describes a small tribe of aborigines. This tribe lives in the vast desert reaches of the Australian outback. There are few of them left, and they live in complete trust of the universe and in harmony with their environment, without tools or any other modern convenience. Marlo became a member of this tribe and hunted, ate, and slept as they did. Everything is scarce where they live, especially food and water. They live completely in the neutral zone, without struggle and effort. They arise every morning with little in the way of supplies and pray for guidance. Every day all of their needs are somehow fulfilled. They are safe and they are supported, in the middle of nowhere, where everything is scarce. If you had no food every morning when you awoke, and there were no restaurants or stores, would you be able to survive? Most of you would not survive. These people have survived for centuries by believing and trusting that they would be taken care of, that their needs would be met.

For most people, having faith seems to require predictable outcomes, yet we all know that the road map of life is constantly changing. We demand consistency, even though we know change is constant. We want the rewards of faith without having to risk loss, asking for mortally measured guarantees from God that our prayers will be answered, our desires fulfilled. Ours is not to know the ways in which God guides our paths, it is enough to know that God will.

In a sense most people have been brainwashed into believing that control and predictability are the only acceptable ways to find happiness in life. In truth, you have another option available. Faith will move you forward because it propels the energy of change. This is a great leap to take because you've been conditioned to believe that the future holds risk. Your task is to dissociate from that belief. If you are willing to go where the divine intelligence of the universe would have you be, you will discover your best possible future. It's entirely up to you to make the effort, to step back from your judgment and decide for yourself what the truth really is.

The truth is subtle. In the world we live in, we have been conditioned to respond only to messages that override our senses, so we often miss anything that isn't louder than the chatter of the ego. Marketers know that in order to get your attention, they have to overwhelm you, and network executives know full well, perhaps too well, the value of shock. Truth, however, comes from the inner world, that place where silence is the backdrop for the wisdom of your soul.

In a world where there is constant change, brought on by modern technology transforming psychological, philosophical, and even religious questions, the truth is often hard to discern, much less to grasp and actually apply in your daily life. As change accelerates, as it is does our time, it tends to create anxieties. People become uneasy because the future seems to become even harder to predict and impossible to secure. Look around. Virtually no one in this society or any western culture trusts life. Everyone locks doors, and in some way builds barricades against intrusion by savages. All who believe they will be violated, will be. When you begin to truly and totally believe you are safe, you create a different dynamic. Inhabiting the neutral zone allows for an entirely new way of being because fear is removed from the equation that is your formula for life.

Pete was a recovering alcoholic. When I met him he had lost everything: his money, his family, his job — all were lost to alcohol and drugs. His guilt and fear about his situation were overwhelming. I encouraged him to meditate and pray, something that he'd never done before. He'd never had any religious training, and he said he wasn't even sure he believed there was a God. Still, what did he have to lose? He earned money by panhandling, slept at a mission at night, and felt only despair. His only place to meditate was on a park bench not far from where he slept. He could not meditate in the shelter because of the noise, and the Christian fundamentalists running the place approved of prayer, but frowned on meditation.

Through Pete's prayer and meditation, his trust and faith began to grow. He expressed his sense that something dramatic was going to happen, although he had no idea what it would be. One day while he was meditating on the bench, a man stopped to talk to him. He told Pete that he'd seen him out there every day and he guessed Pete that was not sleeping, but in an altered state of consciousness. He was a Buddhist who meditated in his office every day at lunch, and he invited Pete to a Buddhist meditation. A few days after Pete attended the meditation, the man offered him a job in a warehouse that his company owned. Pete accepted and now, two years later, he is a shift foreman, who meditates every day during his lunch hour.

As you devote yourself to believing that the grace of God will guide you, the universe will martial its forces to assist you in creating this new reality. When your fears are not blocking the doorway, synchronicity can command your life. Teachers, books, tools and insights will come to you as you are ready, and conditions that allow for the release of your old thought processes will present themselves miraculously. Messages and messengers will arrive to assist you. You may not completely escape your issues without experiencing some of them, but you can definitely shorten the learning curve.

Perhaps, as a business man I would have been more successful had I known this truth at that time, had I been aware of the subtle truths and messages that were constantly presenting themselves to me. Almost everything being done in the business world today is still governed by control and personal will. For ordinary business managers, surrendering and relinquishing the iron fist of control takes a dramatic leap of faith that few are willing to risk. They are mostly still depending upon mission statements and time management techniques to arrive at their goals. What else can you do when you believe you're in charge of your destiny?

As we said before, the only lasting security in life will come from your own faith, your own trust in the universe, and the grace of God. You are always safe. You cannot be harmed. You may discard your body, but your soul is eternal. The life of your soul is an ongoing stream of incarnations. You are here to witness the effects of your choices on yourself and all other life. It is important to know this because it can greatly change the way you judge your experiences. You will learn to believe that you will be safe in the future, even though that knowledge escapes your five senses.

Humans feel separate from everyone and everything in their world. That belief in separation disconnects you from the wisdom of the universe. There are 250 million people in the United States. Imagine what would happen if everyone chose to completely trust in himself and the universe. Like the aboriginal tribe that Marlo Morgan encountered, trust reconnects you not only with the universe, but with everything, including the planet itself. Most people do not realize that they are connected with this planet and all other life forms that inhabit it.

It is through your connection to the earth that you begin to restore balance to all your energies and your life. The separation you perceive is pure fallacy. God, the forest, even trees can and do speak to you. It is only because of your beliefs that you do not hear them. There is a city park in Seattle called Green Lake. Giant old trees have spoken to me on many occasions in this park.

It was late spring 1991. There were still clumps of snow on the ground, covered with pine needles and other debris. Richard Krull and I had decided to go up to Denny Creek in the foothills of the Cascade Mountains. We had been writing, editing and discussing my first book, *Creating your Light Body*. Richard is a man who wears the shirt of mysticism as he moves through his life and is very sensitive and aware of just how alive and conscious the Earth really is.

As we started up the trail, a mile-long trek through the forest along the edge of Denny Creek, I asked Richard, "Can you feel that presence?"

"Yes," he said, "it feels as though a mist has settled around us. Do you know what it is?"

"I think so. It feels very conscious, as though it's trying to communicate with us."

"It is," Richard said. He grew quiet and looked around us, a distant look in his eyes. "It's the consciousness of the land around us."

"What does it want?"

"I'm not sure," Richard replied, "but let's sit on that log over there and I'll see if it can speak through me."

Sitting on a moss-covered log under the canopy of branches, protected by the trees, we felt cool and serene. Richard seemed to blend with and become part of the landscape, and I could sense him deeply absorbed in the dialogue and the experience itself.

"I am indeed the consciousness of this land. This land is a sacred place and has been violated by man. It was an ancient burial site for the native population that once lived in these parts. When the white man came here, he paid little attention to the sacredness of the area or to the spiritual customs of the people that lived here for many years. You can do little about that.

"Over the past 100 years — since this area was logged and clear-cut — it has become a park, a place to come and explore nature, to rest and relax and become more attuned to the river, the trees and the fauna at the edge of the creek.

"The creek is the result of a great subterranean pool that lies beneath these mountains. It is part of what you call your watershed."

"What can we do to help people understand that the earth and the land are a conscious organism?" I asked.

"Help establish more awareness of your connection to the earth. You do not understand that you are part of the planetary system, as much so as the trees and the rocks, rivers and oceans. Assist people in the realization that the earth is alive and must be treated with love and respect. Bring others to this location to share this experience with you. Even those who are already trying to clean up your waste have little understanding of how aware I really am."

It was very still. The only other sound I could hear was the gurgling and splashing of Denny Creek as it sped on down the mountain.

Richard breathed deeply and began again.

"My message to you is that you have too long neglected your home and soiled your nest. But it is not too late to correct what you have done." Richard began to speak haltingly. "The oceans, the forest lands. They are resilient. If you begin now in earnest to save your environment the planet can be saved."

But this is not the only time I had such an experience. One of the most unusual experiences of this nature I have had was when I saw the Chang Dow Dragon, while meditating in the Chang Dow cave in Northern Thailand.

The Chang Dow cave is a fairly typical large cave. It goes back into the hillside about three-quarters of a mile. It has a thirty-foot-high ceiling, bats, and places where if you take the wrong path you will likely never be seen again(which was the fate, not so long ago, of a German tourist). It is dark, damp and smelly. Numerous monks have used the Chang Dow cave as a place of refuge to meditate and pray in. Near the back of the cave there is a stairway to the lower level. The stairway is so steep it might as well be a ladder. There is actually another level even lower than the one we were in, but it is filled with water during the rainy season. This lowest level is reputed to be the home of the Chang Dow dragon.

A group of us, who were on a month-long meditation, went to visit the Chang Dow cave, which is also used as a temple by the local villagers. It is quite a picturesque place, nestled in the arms of a heavily forested mountain near the Burmese border.

We were led through the cave and its many passages by three young Thais with lanterns. At one point during our tour, we had to get down on our hands and knees and crawl through a narrow passage for about ten feet to get to another part of the cave. Water seeped from the walls of the cave in many areas and it smelled of bat guano. Many of us carried flashlights and by pointing them upward we could see the bats on the ceilings. The narrow passage is the only way you can get near the lower level where the dragon is supposed to be. I was somewhat skeptical that such a creature exists. No doubt the Thai version of Bigfoot and the Loch Ness monster, I thought.

I took a seat on a bench that had been carved out of the stone. By that time, we were very experienced meditators and had spent nearly a month in deep meditation. A typical day for us was to get up at 5:00 A.M. and spend the next twelve hours in meditation with forty-five minutes for lunch and then back into meditation.

Within moments I slipped into a deep meditation. Almost immediately I heard what seemed like a cough, but it did not seem human. A chill went up my spine as I wondered where the sound came from. I thought I felt a presence. I opened my eyes but nothing was there. Quickly I closed my eyes again and heard a distinctive roar. There was no mistaking that sound for anything but the roar of a dragon or maybe a stray lion, which was even less likely because there aren't any lions in Southeast Asia.

Suddenly, standing directly in front of me was the Chang Dow dragon. He looked like any other dragon you might see painted on the wall of a Chinese temple, with a face somewhat like a lion, horns, and massive claws. He was a ferocious looking beast, yet love radiated from his eyes.

Startled, I opened my eyes and he was gone. I'd also heard the voice of another dragon, an immature infant. No one had mentioned the existence of a baby dragon, but later on I found out that it also had been heard by others. I closed my eyes and he was back almost immediately. I get it, I thought to myself. This beast lives on the fourth dimension, a dimension higher than we are on, and I can only see him when I am meditating, because in meditation I can easily transcend the third dimension and see into the fourth. It has actually been said that he sometimes manifests on the third dimension.

No doubt many people would reject this out of hand as fantasy. I myself could choose to believe it was simply a hallucination of some sort, but that choice would limit my experience. If you choose to experience higher consciousness and begin to meditate, you will have similar experiences and you'll find them hard to disbelieve. It is faith that opens you to those experiences that will reconnect your awareness to the wisdom of nature, and your link to all life.

In order to regain your trust you must choose to believe differently than you have in the past. That part of you that you call ego absolutely does not want to change. It wants you to operate as you always have. How often do you go over the same ground, rehashing the same problems over and over, attracted to the same experiences and the same types of relationships again and again? You may not enjoy being stuck in the same job or the same old relationship, but it's familiar ground. Changing means relying on the divine intelligence that created all of us in the first place and trusting that something better will come along.

As children we are naturally spontaneous and trusting, but as we grow, limits are placed on what is acceptable. The result is the loss of faith in our own experiences. Certain qualities are not accepted as natural by adults, and because children want to grow up and be accepted by their role models, they learn to disregard who they really are in favor of a more acceptable version. An experienced counselor and psychoanalyst once commented to me that curiosity was not something he often saw in his clients. Spontaneity and curiosity invariably lead to experiences that are beyond the five senses, to paranormal experiences. Of course, children are often ridiculed for believing that such experiences are real.

Often people try to allow just enough awareness into their lives so they can get from one point to another. Guarded awareness, it might be called. Shutting off parts of your experience disconnects you from the guidance of God, while all your ego can do is redirect you back through those old belief systems that created your problems in the first place.

Your soul knows more about running your life or business than you do, because your soul exists beyond polarity. It resides outside of time and space, and is the only part of you that knows what the future looks like. Those gut feelings that have spotted opportunities in the past are your soul communicating with you. Those of you in business may be thinking that all of this is fine and dandy for the average person, but no way are you going to trust that your soul or God can make a good sports shoe, tennis racket, or anything else. You may even demand proof from God of God. But certainly there is ample proof that your current system does not work.

Most business people are highly stressed because they are trying to do everything on their own. Professionals would do much better if they said a simple prayer every morning, asking for guidance to get through the day, and then believed that the answer would arrive. Solutions will come to you if you believe and have faith. Faith is the crucible of change, the alchemy of God.

In his book *Conversations With God,* Neale Donald Walsch addresses this issue by stating that God is always talking to you, and the question is not whether God is speaking to you, but rather, whether you are listening. You may not actually hear the voice of the universe speaking words in your head; few people do. Instead, it may communicate through what you see, what other people say or do, coincidences. Remember that this universe is totally symbolic. All of your outer experience merely reflects your own thinking. Your experience offers answers to every question you hold. In every last detail of the world you witness, there is God speaking to you. Not only do you need to listen with your ears, but you need to become aware with every sense. Once you learn to recognize that your entire world is symbolic, then you will witness the truth of all circumstances.

Trust implies faith in something grander, more intelligent, and wiser than yourself. Begin to have faith in the wisdom of the universe, believing that something divine is guiding your life. You are not alone, abandoned to the vagaries of this world like a ship without a rudder. The universe is constantly giving you life, giving you answers, supporting your being. God constantly speaks with you in one way or another; through feeling, through synchronicity and coincidence, and frequently through other people. A constant barrage of symbols and signposts is there to warn you, and guide you, whispering a future of health, wealth, abundance and love. The mustard seed does not require proof that the sun is shining before it begins to stretch for topsoil. So should you have faith, knowing that you are fully supported in God's function for you. Know that you are safe now and that in the future you always will be safe.

It truly is very simple.

4

Know Thy Self

~ ~ ~ ~ ~ ~ ~ ~ ~ ~ ~ ~ ~ ~ ~ ~

To describe who you are, your strengths, weaknesses, and what motivates your choices, is certainly one of the most challenging things a person can do. But if you don't uncover who you are, life simply becomes a blind acceptance of the way you have been led to believe things are, and you are driven by motives you don't consciously understand. When asked, most people will tell you they understand themselves quite well, but if you ask them if they are completely satisfied with their lives, the answer is no. Of course everyone has some superficial self-knowledge, but the quiet dissatisfaction and stress most people experience speak of a life in which there is constant inner conflict. Knowing yourself means that you understand yourself emotionally, psychologically, physically, and spiritually.

This may seem like a tall order, but it can be accomplished easily if you make the effort one step at a time. Self-awareness progresses like a flower opening to the sun. Your spirituality is at the core of your individuality, and it is the force behind your physical life. But the characteristics of your spiritual self are very different from what you have come to identify with as your physical self. The life force behind the physical expression is what we call soul, and soul is the expression of the even greater life force of God.

As you begin to know and understand yourself, you have to explore the nature of your soul and its relationship to God and to your physical life here on earth. People take on the challenge of knowing and understanding themselves for any number of reasons. Most people are motivated to understand themselves better because something seems to have gone wrong in their lives. They don't have enough money or love, they are experiencing painful emotions as in the breakup of a relationship, etc.

Some are motivated out of physical problems they are facing. Finding that their physical problems don't respond to treatment, they're prompted to explore the psychological aspects of disease. Early in this century, modern medicine established a category of psychosomatic health problems, and then systematically discredited or chose to ignore the effects of emotions, thoughts, and feelings in the process of disease. This is an incredibly limited view of disease and illness. Obviously, disease has an impact on emotions, so why can't emotions affect disease? Perhaps modern medicine has tried to ignore that connection because if the doctors give it credence they'll have to explore their own emotional makeup. Few people are willing to do that exploration.

The courage to do so speaks highly of your inner strength. Exploring who you are inevitably creates change, and humans deplore change. Yet they demand change from the outer world. Most people would prefer that the changes in their lives come about because others have changed their response to them, rather than changing anything about themselves.

This externalized view of the world is one perpetuated by societies all over the world. It ignores the possibility that just maybe *you* are creating, all by yourself, the world you see around you. A popular book from a number of years ago was titled *You'll See It When You Believe It*. Put simply, if examined, what we see is the result of what we believe about the world we live in. So if you see the world as a wonderful, joyous, abundant place, that is what you will experience. If you see life as a struggle filled with disappointment and lack, then that is what you will experience.

Understanding your own self creates a foundation for you to build your life upon, much like the foundation your home is built upon. In most locales you can't get a permit to build a house that doesn't have a strong foundation, nor can you obtain a mortgage or insurance for any kind of building that lacks a proper foundation. Most people attempt to build the "house" of their life without giving thought to a strong foundation, and then they wonder why there is so much unmanageable stress in it. Your life is your own creation. If you don't have a strong foundation from spiritual understanding, you'll only be building a house of cards that will tumble with the slightest breeze.

You may begin your self-exploration on the physical, emotional, psychological, or spiritual level. If your intent is to know yourself, the doors will automatically open for you. In Cathy Lee Crosby's book, *Let the Magic Begin,* she shares that she was intent on gaining knowledge about diet and exercise. She stopped into a bookstore and, quite by accident, was guided by the bookstore owner to explore books about spirituality. Like many others, she discovered that you cannot build an adequate foundation and make lasting improvements in your life without exploring all facets of your self. The psychoanalytical community tried for years to assist people in healing their psyches without exploring spiritual issues. Since then many mainstream psychologists have begun teaching about spirituality as part of therapy. Currently, you can even obtain a Ph.D. from many universities in transpersonal psychology, which addresses spiritual issues and values. Obviously, the psychological community has finally recognized the benefits of a spiritual knowledge of oneself to one's overall well-being.

You explore your spiritual nature because it is the basis from which all life emerges. This exploration and understanding gives you a new perspective on your own physical life, and understanding your spirituality gives you abilities and tools you'll need if you wish to survive this lifetime. Your spiritual self, soul, or whatever you wish to call it may lead you to entirely new choices in your life. We all make choices, but often those choices are motivated by the subconscious desires of your ego. Ego's needs are based on the past, based on the belief that something which was missing in the past will fill its needs. Your soul has no such needs created by past experience. Soul will guide you to the best experience possible for you at any given time. It knows which choices will produce the best results for you in the long run.

The creation of your life is all about choices. You have the ability to choose whatever experiences you would like. Many, of course, make a choice that doesn't work and then blame someone else or some outside event for the results. You can stop that blaming by turning inward and uncovering the reasons and the motivations behind your actions. To know thy self is such a natural quality that if you sit down, close your eyes and focus your attention inward, you'll obtain any knowledge of yourself that you seek.

If you're unwilling to take these simple steps, you may as well throw this book away and carry on the way you have been. Better yet, give this to someone who is willing to do what you are not. Sooner or later, whether in this lifetime or another, you will have to turn inward, but it won't and can't happen until you are ready. Many people have to hit bottom before seeking to know what motivates their choices. I hope this doesn't apply to you. Most people put very little effort into knowing themselves or believing in who they are, yet the rewards of such effort are phenomenal.

If your life isn't working, it is because you haven't looked within. You can pay lip service to knowing that still, small inner voice and you may know all the right things to say, but if you're still struggling against circumstances, you haven't truly turned inward. This book is about the basics. When you practice the fundamentals, growth and change will become a way of life. Your awareness will expand, encompassing more of God's creation, and you will know exactly what to do next in any situation. You will begin to live from the neutral zone, outside of polarity, and everything you need will come your way with little or no effort. And isn't that what you really want? To stop struggling?

Up to this point, you have most likely identified with your personality and accepted its limiting beliefs about the nature of the reality you live in, although you really have not had much choice in the matter. As a child, you were spoon fed the version of reality your parents believed to be true. Schools, institutions, and even your peers reinforced that belief. As your personality took on those attitudes and beliefs it became invested in them and learned to protect them like a lion protects a kill, and with about the same finesse.

In this day and age many people are searching for spiritual growth. Exploration of your self is not done simply for the sake of exploration, but so that obstacles, issues and fears can be overcome and released. Knowing your self is clearing the self. The light of awareness will quickly dissolve those areas where you find yourself stuck. Self-exploration is a skill you can learn. The more you practice, the better you'll become at listening to the wisdom of your own soul. There is a universal principle you need to know that is also generally agreed on in mainstream psychology: You will never be given more than you can handle. That means you will never be truly overwhelmed by what you find buried in your psyche. Anything that comes up as dysfunctional motivation or reasoning will also be within your ability to overcome. The feeling of being over-whelmed is merely a ploy stemming from your ego's resis-tance to change. Remember, it thinks it is doing you a favor by keeping you stuck in the familiar.

There is a category of issues which can be very debil-itating that I have not seen discussed elsewhere. I call them subconscious contracts, or agreements, that you have with your family members. For example, you may make a subconscious contract not to be more successful than your parents. You might also unknowingly make a contract to carry on behavioral family traditions such as abuse, neglect, denial, and poverty. Your family heritage goes back genera-tions and is brought to you at your cellular and genetic levels. Your ancestors invested a great deal of effort and energy in it and they and your present family identify with

it. The family drama is deeply embedded and rarely ques-
tioned. You may be totally unaware of your agreement to
fulfill those familial patterns, but you will pass them on to
the next generation just as your parents did. After all, the
family cherishes its traditions, even the negative ones,
because they are safe and familiar. Only those who are
willing to go inward and explore the depths of their own
psyches will break these patterns. Your family will not like
you exposing their secrets and you'll run into all sorts of
opposition, but it is the only way you can stop buying into
their dysfunctional behavior.

Susan had a master's degree in architecture. She was
the most educated person in her family, the only one ever to
attend college. In the various companies she worked for,
anytime she was up for a promotion something would get in
the way. Often, it was a physical problem that kept her away
from work for long periods, sometimes several months. By
the time she came to see me she was already looking for
work in a different field.

She blamed the dissatisfaction that she felt about her
career on her career choice. Like so many other people, she
had decided that forces beyond her control were playing on
her life. As we explored her inner world we found that she
subconsciously had formed contracts with the members of
her family that would not allow her to show them up. For
her, the strongest agreement was with her older sister. This
was her way of placating an older sister when she was very
young, but it had carried over into her adult life as contracts
children make so often do. Once she became aware of the
problem, she was able to overcome it and get on with her
life.

The most difficult exploration usually occurs when
you explore your emotions. In this culture, we are great

suppressors of emotions and feeling. Both men and women have been taught that emotions are somehow bad, or harmful. Yet studies on crying show that there is a tremendous relief of tension and anxiety as a result of the simple act of crying. Anyone who has explored emotional release can attest to the catharsis that occurs when deeply suppressed emotions surface and are experienced.

The psychological community has, for some time, divided people into two categories: neurotic and characterlogical. Those who are neurotic respond to standard therapy techniques, but those who are characterlogical do not. Characterlogical people are more outwardly focused than others and often demonstrate anger, whereas neurotics have more fear and focus on what they think is wrong with themselves. It is also my experience that characterlogical types are often in denial that there is anything wrong with their approach to life, blaming others for their problems. Those who are angry are blocked from awareness until their anger is released, and some of those who are the most angry are not even aware of it. They spend a great deal of their lives in ways that keep them from having to explore that aspect of themselves. If you are characterlogical, subtle introspective therapies probably will not work for you, but something dynamic that is designed to bring up your emotions can quickly move you through your anger so that you can release it.

As I have traveled the planet, and worked with, taught, and participated in both small and large groups of people, it has become clear to me that almost everyone in the western world is suppressing emotions and feelings. The origin of this behavior is not well understood, but was once explained to a group of students by Leslie Temple Thurston, an enlightened westerner whose wisdom is amazing! She said that as a result of a child not getting enough love it changes focus from the heart center, or heart chakra, to the third chakra, the seat of anger and personal will. Very few, if any, children receive enough love from their parents. How can they when church, careers, school, and outside activities occupy so much of parents' and children's time, especially in the western world.

As you evolve, you give up your personal will. If you are strong-willed and ego-centered, you most likely are affronted by the thought of giving up your personal will. Almost everyone believes that success is dependent upon personal strength, will, persuasion, or other qualities of personality. It is not. Your success in this world is much more dependent upon your self-awareness than any qualities of the personality. After all, isn't it logical to think that a man who struggles as an accountant — regardless of vast force of will and determination to make it as an accountant — would have been better off if he'd discovered that his natural aptitude was more toward art and literature rather than cold hard numbers? That's why inner qualities such as intuition are far more critical to your ultimate success. But these can easily be blocked by your emotions and personal will. Will and anger often occupy the same space in your energy system, your third chakra. Many people will try to circumvent this aspect of growth and maturity, but everyone has to grow up sometime and stop blaming the world for his or her plight.

Self-awareness does not come cheap. It requires an investment of energy and a dedication to knowing your self. This is the real work of the spiritual warrior, as well as those who wish for true success in their lives. The good news is that knowing your self is not all hard work. Sometimes great inspiration comes as the result of the simple act of contemplation, meditation, or even daydreaming. This book came to me after completing a half-hour meditation. Your commitment and the intent to know your self will bring to the surface any blocks you may have.

You cannot explore your self without turning inward, and there is always the chance that you will find deeply buried emotions, memories, even traumatic events, that you would rather not look at. However, you are just as likely to find marvelous, wonderful qualities, and aspects of your self that you did not know were there. For example, it never occurred to me that I could be a writer until I began deeply exploring my inner nature. This is my third book. It is a great source of creative experience that lay completely dormant until I began to explore my self and my feeling nature. The deeper meaning for your own life may very well be suppressed with your feelings.

Your reason for living on this emerald-green planet is in truth a divine plan. You are here with the skills, abilities, aptitudes, and whatever else it takes not only to survive this life, but to prosper as well. You are like no other. You are unique, and you have unique skills and abilities. They may be shrouded, obscured, and denied, but they are there. What seems to plague many individuals is a sense of being hope-lessly flawed, perhaps the only mistake God ever made. This is just a clever ruse of the ego designed to make you feel special, and to keep you that way — especially stuck and attached to your personal will.

I have never met anyone who, exploring her unique-ness, did not begin to take on the qualities of a saint, or a Christ. It is perhaps fleeting at first, but nevertheless those qualities begin to emerge. You may never have thought of uncovering your own saintly nature, but it is there. Like so many other parts of you, it is simply buried under a lot of debris. Does it shock you to think there may be a saint in you? Did your ego tell you, "Oh, that's ridiculous!"? Then that's a sure sign that your ego is working against you. That's okay. It's just going to take some time, because maybe you aren't ready to accept that just yet. But take heart, because you'll soon be like the many others who have discovered great latent qualities and gifts, and will soon be digging even deeper to see what else is there.

Your soul's joy and happiness come from experiencing your soul's uniqueness. Self-awareness unlocks your soul's gifts. It is that uniqueness that you're trying to uncover, along with its connection to the universe and the divine. That is the channel you are trying to reconnect with, because by doing so you tap into a much larger reservoir of potentials, skills, and aptitudes. Your higher nature is far more adept at surviving your life than ego could ever be.

You can explore the inner sanctum of your psyche and find your real power and creativity. You can know yourself and perfect the art of awareness. You don't need to go to counselors and therapists to begin to discover who you are. Knowing yourself is simply a metaphor for raising consciousness and connecting with your soul. The selves you find along the way are really only relative selves, relative selves that have been trained in this third-dimensional reality. To a large degree, they will be transient. They'll hang around for a while, and then you'll release that self and explore yet another layer of truth as you move closer to your soul and God.

5

Money

~ ~ ~ ~ ~ ~ ~ ~ ~ ~ ~ ~ ~ ~ ~

Much of the current material you read about prosperity will tell you that your Creator wants you to experience abundance (usually translated as material wealth), and obviously God didn't want you to be destitute. But your survival in life is related to things far removed from making money. You can easily make more money than you do presently, simply by applying the principles in this chapter. However, if you desire fulfillment and satisfaction as well as money, you will have to create a new way of thinking about money. You'll need a new philosophical base from which you can revamp your subconscious beliefs about money. If you are surviving at a subsistence level and aren't satisfied or fulfilled by your life, then the major culprit is something within your psyche that prevents you from having more — more money, more love, and more of everything. The purpose of life is self-discovery. As you travel the path of self-discovery, you'll uncover the reason or reasons why you don't have more of what you desire in your life.

When you look around and see those who have more than you do for no apparent reason, it isn't because they're smarter or luckier than you. That has nothing to do with it. Being wealthy or affluent often is the result of your soul's desire for you in this lifetime, the result of having a fortuitous program for this lifetime. Your program for this life is your karmic imprint, which includes the goals within your reach. If that imprint contains being wealthy as a likelihood, then you can probably manifest money with relative ease. Of course, you may also have to remove some obstacles and issues that you've created, in order to reach that goal. Overcoming those obstacles may indeed be more important to your soul than becoming wealthy. In fact, once you've reached a certain point in your growth, the allure of wealth will dissipate.

During a cycle of incarnations you will experience nearly all conditions; wealth, poverty, power, and even homelessness. Every incarnation is designed to accommodate greater understanding and awareness of the material world, and to balance and integrate polarity.

It is very likely that if you have experienced being wealthy in a recent lifetime, it will not be part of your path in this lifetime. The desire for wealth can also be only your ego's desire and have little to do with what your soul truly wants.

Most readers who read this will probably not be interested in joining the ranks of the super rich, but rather in following a path of joy and fulfillment that includes having your needs met. Great wealth is so distracting that it is rarely included in a lifetime where an individual soul seeks to reach higher levels of consciousness.

In this culture you can acquire money by blindly following the crowd, but one of the biggest mistakes you can make is to blindly follow the crowd. The media, schools, your parents and friends will encourage you to take part in whatever is the latest economic trend. One decade it's MBAs, the next it's software engineers, and the next it's something entirely different. If you really feel drawn to one of those fields don't ignore that feeling, but make sure it is your desire and not that you are simply being drawn in by hype and the force of the crowd. The lure of big bucks seduces many. Unless it leads to satisfaction and fulfillment, the work you do will have little real value to you. The most nourishing path will be to follow your soul's desire for you. Your soul may be a bit of a taskmaster in this regard, stopping your life until you consider its needs.

Many people refer to this falling away of life as they know it as the "dark night of the soul," although for most it takes longer than a single night. My own dark night of the soul lasted for four and a half years. My marriage broke up, and my business life simply fell apart. I lived in a ramshackle tenement. I didn't even own a car. After earning millions in business, I barely had enough money for bus fare, and I often wondered if I would end up living on the streets. At this point I began to turn inward for resources, which is the whole reason one experiences the dark night of the soul. The same message came to me over and over again during all this: pray, meditate, and clear the blocks to growth and prosperity; trust, allow, have faith, stay centered and in this moment. If I heard the message one more time, I might have killed the messenger — at least I felt that way at times! During that period I screamed and shouted at God. I cried, wailed, kicked, screamed, tried to practice the principles presented in this book and faithfully continued to meditate and clear my self. And through it all, the message kept coming to me: "You will have what you desire, success and fulfillment. Just keep the faith."

In order for you to survive this lifetime you will need to explore your role in this life, because it is therein that you will find fulfillment. The more you know about your role, the quicker and easier it will be for you to make the changes needed to become aligned with your soul's purpose. Your program for this lifetime was set in place — chosen, if you will — by your soul in order to facilitate its own experience, growth and evolution. After all, your soul is the lone survivor of each one of your lifetimes. Ego and body turn to dust.

Money, as some would describe it, is simply a medium of exchange, but it is much more. It is a direct reflection of love. When you are living in harmony with your soul's desire, money will flow freely, as does love. By the same token, when you are at odds with who you are, the flow of money in your life is restricted. This point should not be overlooked. Money is a spiritual commodity, and you are rewarded by following a path that puts you into alignment with spiritual principles and your soul's desires. When you do not have enough money, it means you are out of alignment with your soul's plan for this lifetime. When you are centered in the neutral zone and acting out of your inner wisdom, your soul can speak to you and realign you with your ability to create wealth and abundance. Thus, maintaining a connection with your inner wisdom is the most important thing you can do to increase your prosperity.

Believe me, it took a tremendous amount of faith and trust on my part to get through that dark period of my life. From time to time I rebelled, but try as I might I could not move out of that void by force of my own personal will.

After a lifetime of initiating successful business ventures, I couldn't get anything off the ground.

Nearly everyone goes through a time like this at some point in life, especially those who are committed to their spiritual growth. It forces them to look to God for answers. During my dark time, I always had enough to eat and a roof over my head. During these dark times you learn to stand alone in your own integrity and power, because the soul that cannot stand alone can do little for another. They are periods of gestation in which you are preparing at deep inner levels for flight. Much like the butterfly symbolizes spirituality, during these periods you are transforming toward the next stage of your spiritual evolution. Generally, this feels like punishment to the personality, as if perhaps you are being thwarted for unrepented sins. This is not completely true. These periods of gestation mark an inter-section in time and space when a great spiritual being can emerge. If you have had the experience of the worldly life falling away and have gone through a time of drought when the landscape is barren, you have passed through the dark night of the soul and will be forever changed. The world as you once knew it will slide into the past, and you will see everything in life in a new light, a light that offers more hope, more love, and more success.

What happens during these times is that you clear many issues which have been blocking the success you so desire. You are shedding the skin of the outer world, preparing for union with your soul and God. While it may be very frustrating to the conscious mind, it is very rewarding on inner levels, where your soul is nurtured. For some people, this clearing is not done on a conscious level. You find yourself being propelled in a new direction and unable to prevent it. You will know it is the right path because in spite of your not being sure what is going on, it will simply feel right.

For example, during my own dark night, I would wake up some mornings and swear I would start selling real estate again out of desperation. By mid-1997, I could still see no signs of improvement. Then, late in June, I attended a workshop to become a facilitator of a new and exciting process. I had made plans to go to Thailand, but upon my return from this workshop, I canceled those plans. I was not sure how this would cure my impending financial ills, but I just felt it was the right thing to do. God and my higher self were telling me to stay put.

Suddenly, the synchronicity became apparent and everything fell into place. A friend of mine who works for a locally published metaphysical newspaper asked me for an interview about this new process I had learned. Things seemed to go awry when the publishing of the interview was delayed for one month, but as a result of that, the article appeared on the front page instead of buried inside. This prominent display, the result of unseen hands, resulted in a great amount of feedback and support from across the country.

Your inner child's attitudes about money are also important because they dictate your true feelings about money. Your inner child will very often take on the beliefs about money that your parents held. My own father thought that all businessmen were crooks, so my having money came with the stigma of being dishonest. Typically, conscious desire will not be enough to override the attitudes of your inner child. Fortunately, your inner child is not speechless. Through journaling and other methods (regression hypnotherapy, etc.) your inner child can speak those beliefs and fears that hold you back, which is exactly what those limiting beliefs will do until they are discovered and purged.

Money comes quickly and easily if nothing is standing in the way. Contrary to popular belief, having abundance has nothing to do with hard work and struggle. It has everything to do with how you feel about being prosperous. If you've been struggling and poor for a long time, chances are that your ego has become identified with struggle and poverty and will resist change. In a sense, you become addicted to your way of life. Your ego will attempt to support your old, familiar way of life through your thoughts, words, and deeds. This is why monitoring your thoughts is perhaps the most important part of the process of change. Sometimes your thoughts are the result of a deeply rooted belief that will have to be identified and changed. Your success is dependent upon your ability to let go of the belief that all the chatter of the ego is real. The only power fear has is power you willingly give to it.

Thoughts are things. They are self-fulfilling prophecies. Those that are habitual for you have a strong tendency to appear as events in your life. Surely you have heard this before, so why is it so hard to understand? Because of your judgment and polarization. Your likes and dislikes and your ego's addiction to the drama you call your life — these are the problems. How attached you have become to your dramas, how you love to tell and retell the history of your past, wallowing in it! As surely as you have created everything in your life thus far, you can create something better. You can choose to create differently. When? You can start now, but it takes commitment.

Life is a co-creative process, or at least it could be, and probably works with a great deal more ease when it is lived in harmony with God. This is all your soul truly desires; it is aiming for harmonious existence. Money, of course, comes as a result of being in that harmony. God will begin to deliver what you need, when you need it, when you are in a state of harmony and surrender. The degree to which your prosperity is related to your alignment with your spirit's values cannot be overemphasized. Your ego may want to control this aspect of your life, to be in charge of the realm of your economic well-being. Regardless, your financial destiny will not be the result of your ego's desires. Sooner or later your spirit will have its say and get its way.

The universe will never argue with you over the choices you make in life. You can do whatever you want to do. It is simply easier for God to assist you when you are in alignment with your blueprint for this lifetime. What God wants is for you to have everything you choose to have. But you must look at why you do what you do, what motivates your choices, and what your focus is on. Focusing on the future may be self-defeating because the personality/ego rarely knows which future choices will put you into alignment with your higher needs. Your ego knows what it thinks it wants, and not much else. Instead, discover your purpose, find the best way to fulfill that purpose, then focus on your life moment by moment and you will be rewarded.

There is absolutely nothing that can stop you from having a life of bliss and joy, except your own fear. Those who are unwilling to face their fears are doomed to continually create them because they will grow in the darkness of denial and suppression. If you choose to ignore your negative beliefs, then they will manifest. Many people get stuck in their beliefs and attitudes, becoming locked into a downward spiral. Money comes to you not out of your desire for money but as the result of being available to universal consciousness and allowing it to flow through you, which occurs only when you are in the neutral zone and not polarized.

Love is the most valuable quality there is. Love creates the widest pathway for more money and any other conditions you desire to come to you. This is loudly proclaimed in a book entitled *Do What You Love and the Money Will Follow*. Love and gratitude are energetic states and they attract similar energies. Money comes out of the energy of love, gratitude, and other positive feelings. Likewise, it is repelled by fear and other negative energies. The universe is a generous place and will hold nothing back from you, but there are universal principles that guide this planet. The most important of these is that your inner beliefs about the world truly do create the world you witness. They dictate what you see or focus on in the outer world, and are redirected back to you in spades. Focus is the most important aspect of achievement of any kind. What you focus your attention on increases. Whether positive or negative in nature, conscious or subconscious, focus and desire will move mountains. In a linear reality things can take time to manifest in your life. When you focus on the essence of something rather than its physical appearance, it will speed the process. For instance, if you want a nice home, acquiring the money to purchase one may take longer than being open to the possibility of someone allowing you to live in their home while they travel around the world.

Not only your thoughts but your feelings as well are manifested in your outer world. Feelings are the energizer, the emotive force. It seems as though things come to us out of the blue, but everything comes as a result of energy and attention focused toward a possibility. By the time I was twenty years old I knew that I wanted to be wealthy, and — just like in my search for the meaning of life — I sought and devoured any information I could find on getting rich. I ate, slept and breathed the possibility of becoming wealthy.

Money can be a false idol. You simply must be in alignment with your soul to be happy and fulfilled. I desired wealth, I desired economic power, but it was not enough. Until I integrated the power of spirit into my life, I was unfulfilled. Nevertheless, I made a great deal of money by following the simple rules of manifestation. I was highly focused, highly motivated, and that was all it took. You can do the same, but you must be prepared to persist in your desire to accomplish what it is your soul wishes. I love the quote from Napoleon Hill, author of *Think and Grow Rich,* who said, "Persistence is to man as carbon is to steel." Carbon, of course, gives steel its strength.

Almost everyone wants to make achievement complicated, but it is a simple process. Focus on what you want, and then remove the obstacles that stand between you and the desired condition. If you choose to have faith and trust, and work with your angels and guides toward fulfilling your soul's desire, joy and abundance will be a natural result. The thoughts and pictures you hold in your imagination, combined with an intense feeling, be it fear or love, will indeed manifest.

The point is this: Everyone is a good manifester or creator. You create what you do not want because of your fear and ignorance. Once you understand what it is that holds you back, you can change. It is fear, of course, that holds you back because it blocks your communication with your higher nature. Much of your fear is disguised as negative thoughts about yourself: I could never do that because I am too old, too fat, too short; I come from the wrong side of the tracks; I don't know the right people; I am not smart enough to do that, I'm not creative enough, and don't have enough education; my children are holding me back, I am responsible for them, who'd take care of them?

These fears and limitations are not real, they're learned.

When you absolutely cannot see a way out, that is the time to pray for God's help. With all those negative thoughts, beliefs, and fears you'll never be able to figure it out on your own.

You are always learning, changing and growing. It is as natural as the change of the seasons, but you must be free to evolve in the direction your spirit desires. That means you must remove the roadblocks that are keeping you from finding meaning in your life. There are many who cannot enjoy what they are doing even though it could be very satisfying, because of the chaos in their emotional bodies. Such chaos is always the result of fear. When you perceive life as threatening, joy and fulfillment will be hard to find amidst the chaos.

The energy of feelings is the energy that creates. It is the intensity of a desire that manifests what you want. This is why when you are in great fear about a possibility, focusing on the fear only attracts it. By the same token, what your heart desires is already yours, and it lies in wait for you to act toward it. Nothing can stop you from achieving what you believe you can have. There is a saying: What the mind of man can conceive and believe, he can achieve. If you can imagine having something, you can have it all, although perhaps not instantaneously. You will discover that when you move into the neutral zone, outside of polarity and judgment, change will come quickly in many areas of your life. Synchronicity will begin to work overtime for you. The higher you climb up the ladder of consciousness, the easier all of this gets. This means that if you are doing the necessary clearing work, meditating a few half-hours or more weekly, then the universe will become more involved with you. Then you need do very little to reap the rewards you seek, which is why it becomes so very important for you to stay out of the polarity of judgment and in the neutral zone.

The universe is self-correcting. It is always trying to achieve balance and harmony. So once you accept your soul's desire, the natural tendency of the universe is to reflect that back at you. The more committed you are to aligning yourself with your soul, the more assistance you will receive. You will move quickly along the path of change. But if you choose to remain in denial and not look at the issues related to your lack, the conditions of your life will only get worse. Energetically, you are always in motion, in a state of flux. You will either be reinforcing the old beliefs in lack and poverty, or you will be releasing them and moving rapidly ahead toward balance, harmony and prosperity.

I have used a number of different modalities for clearing my own blocks: psychoanalysis, rebirthing (an excellent technique that uses breathing to release suppressed emotions and feelings), hypnotherapy, contemplation, and journaling, which is a very simple and effective technique — all you need is paper and pencil. Journaling should be done in times of quiet introspection, when you can let your inner self set up the dialogue. You will be amazed at what comes forth. Journaling also has the added benefit of being free because you don't need a professional facilitator.

If you're a beginner or have just started to explore these concepts, you may feel overwhelmed by all of this. The first stage is the most difficult because you are just beginning to change those entrenched beliefs about the way things work. The best advice I can give you is to keep reading, look for like-minded people to discuss these issues with, and every so often come back to the basics, here or elsewhere. It will not be long before your new belief system takes hold and begins to redirect your life.

God could care less whether you choose to be rich or poor. God simply gives you every option, unlimited choices. Which choices you make is entirely up to you. There is virtually nothing for you to do except set sail and let the currents of the universe carry you out to what it knows will be the most fulfilling place for you in this lifetime. In that perfect place for you, you will be completely supported, and money will cease to be an issue.

6

Purpose

~ ~ ~ ~ ~ ~ ~ ~ ~ ~ ~ ~ ~ ~ ~

In all of creation, nothing is without function. To find meaning and satisfaction in this lifetime, you'll have to come into alignment with your purpose, and fulfilling your purpose is one of the simplest and most rewarding things you can do, for that is what your soul intends. Many people spend a great deal of their lives in search of their life's purpose, claiming that they'd be happy if only they could find it. If it's that important, then why haven't they found it?

If your life is not working it's because you're out of alignment with your purpose. Even though you say you want to discover your purpose, you may not be willing to face the changes this would entail. What many people are really looking for is a way to satisfy the ego's version of what it thinks it needs to be happy. This is often a far cry from what the soul needs, and it doesn't include a lot of, if any, change. Ego will accept gradual change, but if finding purpose means radical change then there will be a lot of resistance to finding your purpose.

My forthrightness may seem a little harsh to you, but this is the conclusion I've come to after years of working with people on this issue. Many people will go so far as to commit suicide rather than face their need to change. It takes great courage to change because to do so you need to stop blaming others for the circumstances in your life. This is not something most of us do easily.

John came to me because he was very dissatisfied with his job as a gardener. It didn't pay him well enough, but he did enjoy it. During the course of his one-hour session, we learned that working as a gardener was indeed in line with his purpose in this lifetime. His purpose was to cultivate a deep connection with the earth, and he did this by gardening. One of the options he considered was working as a salesman for a wholesale gardening company. Doing so would keep him in touch with the plants and flow of life on earth. Not everyone is so lucky. For John, this was a minor change that still kept him in alignment with his purpose for this lifetime, as well as affording him a better life.

A friend of mine in his late twenties was rather despondent when I first met him because he was tired of dead-end jobs. One thing he was very skilled at and loved to do was writing, but he was unable to make a living as a writer. Someone offered him the opportunity to work on a book that was the true story of a man who relived memories from the life of Saul of Tarsus. After completing work on the book, my friend had a vision of one of his past lifetimes. He visited a hypnotherapist and ended up going through two past-life regression sessions with her. During those visits a lifetime of great significance came forward, and he discovered that one of his purposes in this lifetime was to write about that lifetime.

Purpose is such an integral part of the life your soul signed up for, that if given even the slightest chance, your purpose will find you. Being in alignment with your purpose creates a life that is satisfying, fulfilling and abundant. If you are feeling anything less, you haven't found your purpose, and if you aren't receiving an adequate reward for what you're doing, something is wrong. Purpose always includes prosperity, or at least a comfortable living. That is to say, once you are fulfilling your purpose, you'll realize that you're perfectly supported and provided for.

We live compartmentalized lives; work is one thing, play another, relationships yet another. When you're in alignment with your purpose, work becomes play, struggle ceases and your life blossoms effortlessly. All of your activity becomes a communion with spirit, a demonstration of love, which adds a whole new dimension to the dance of your life.

Finding purpose is simply discovering your own uniqueness. Whatever your contribution is intended to be, it will be a highly-sought-after quality because only you will have that quality, knowledge, and ability. This is your indi- viduality, the one thing that makes you unlike any other. Of course it may be an entire gestalt of qualities, a combination of attributes and skills found nowhere else on earth. This may seem far-fetched, but it is true. You are unique. There is no one else like you on this planet or anywhere in all of the universe, nor has there ever been someone exactly like you.

Some of these qualities will be obvious to you if you give it some consideration. Others will be more obscure and you will have to go inward to find them. Your purpose may look mundane or esoteric. For instance, you might be one of the army of people who have incarnated to support the computer industry. It is still new and needs imaginative, creative people like you for support and to discover new applications for its use. Some people that do computer work might think their work is mundane, but that is only because they haven't discovered the way in which their own uniqueness and purpose apply to their work. Discovering your purpose may literally lead you to a new world, a different lifestyle in a different place, surrounded by different people. Keep in mind that it is futile to let your ego dictate a career change. Being born of your past, ego is very limited in its creative abilities. Until you discover what your soul's purpose is, you will simply end up doing the same dissatisfying work.

Your purpose may be very narrow or very broad in its scope. It is not enough that you simply find your function; you need to uncover the means to actualize your purpose. For instance, if you have a general purpose like exploring form, you could do that as an architect, draftsman, or carpenter. The sub-purpose might be the need to work with your hands, if you were to become a draftsman or carpenter. But if part of your purpose is to work with logic and analysis, you should probably be an architect. Once you realize why you are here, you'll find that you are a highly creative person relative to your purpose, and you will be filled with ideas and inspiration.

Imagine how the world would look if everyone were to discover their own uniqueness and purpose. No one would be hungry, homeless or unemployed. Humanity would evolve beyond imagination. As it is, many industries are stalled or failing. They cannot make any forward progress until the right person supplies them with some unique quality or information. That is how important your contribution can be. Every invention existed as an idea first. Look at your surroundings wherever you are right now and consider the marvelous demonstration of individual purpose fulfilled, and creativity expressed, that makes up our modern world: the intricate machinations of the automobile, microwave ovens, Teflon, synthetics, vegetable oil, refrigeration, and every implement you utilize in your life.

You are a spiritual being whether you acknowledge it or not. Knowing why you are here comes from the spiritual understanding and connection you must have with your own soul, and with God. Once you look within to find your heart's desire, it cannot be missed. Your purpose is encoded in your energies and cellular structure. It colors every part of your makeup: biologically, energetically, emotionally, and genetically. You are not your ego and personality, that is simply the stance you are taking in this lifetime because of your cultural training. You could just as easily have been taught something else. You could have been taught the truth of who you are, the truth that you are self-sufficient. You are a spiritual being disguised as a human being. You have been created in the image and likeness of God, and inherent in that likeness is everything you need to be a living god on Earth — everything you need to be totally connected to your purpose, soul, and God.

This is not a new thought. It was recorded 2,000 years ago, but like all simple truths the meaning has been lost. If you can accept that your life has a higher purpose, then it follows that you also have the potential to actualize that purpose. There are many levels of your purpose here. On the human level, every soul incarnates with a program — some areas of existence in which it would like to increase its knowledge, experience, and understanding.

A Course in Miracles makes it very clear that there are no special souls, that we are all created equally. Yet, each one of us is entirely unique. It is this uniqueness that will be your greatest tool. It is God's gift to you. Successful people everywhere have used their individual uniqueness to build the foundations of their lives. A neighbor and friend of mine, who was seventy years old at the time, had the unique ability to make wooden boats. Even though he made small wooden boats suitable for only one or two fishermen, he could not build them fast enough. Local fishermen bought them as quickly as he could build them. He had retired from his career, yet found himself busier than ever and loving it, because he was doing what he loved. You can make your uniqueness an asset available for the benefit of others. Of course, you will have to uncover it, and to do that you will have to go inward.

My own purpose in this lifetime was exemplified for me at an early age. By the time I was twenty-six, I was part owner of one of the most successful fitness centers in America. When I began to lose money three years later, I left the business feeling very bad about the outcome. After that I owned a real estate company and a restaurant. My next venture was perhaps the most disappointing of all. I started a carpet cleaning company with two employees, and three years later had four hundred people working for me all over the country. After five or six years of tremendous success, it also began to fail.

These failures always contained a similar thread, unbeknown to me at the time: I was self-destructive and chose business partners with the same neurotic pathology. It is a universal principle that you will always attract people to you to demonstrate your inner pathology until you release the issue.

It took me a number of years to become aware of what the problem was. It was a learning deficit, not a physical one but an inner one. I have subsequently discovered that anyone who is listening to his or her inner wisdom and voice will always know what to do and when to do it. My CPA had warned me not to expand so fast; my wife at the time suggested a different course of action; someone offered to buy me out; and my inner voice spoke to me about not staying in this business for more than five or six years. All of this went unheard by me.

Why was I so unable to hear what people and that inner voice were saying? Because as a child, I'd learned that I could not trust others and I had to rely on only myself to survive. This was the result of an abusive childhood.

Those failures caused me to search for the meaning to my life and have resulted in an understanding of the spiritual, psychological, emotional and physical reasons for my being here. This is something I probably wouldn't have been motivated to search for had I not first experienced the success and the subsequent failures. Indeed, God works in strange and mysterious ways.

Any information regarding your own purpose is available to you as you go inward. An inability to find it simply means you need to do more clearing work. The complete picture might come to you all at once, or over a period of time. As you raise your consciousness, your purpose may even change. That is what happened to me, although I use a lot of the same abilities for writing that I used in business. I also sense that sometime soon I will find out more about yet a new purpose for me.

At some point in your evolution, your purpose will include stewardship of the planet. Everyone is connected to the planet in some way, but as you evolve you become more aware of your connection to planetary energy systems. Humans are inherently part of the ecosystem of the planet. You may not initially be aware of your role with the planet, but as you evolve it will emerge. We have come to an intersection in time on this planet when it is not enough to simply deal with the human purpose of your soul being here on earth. Humanity is running out of time. We all must learn to have a more cosmic view, a reconnection with our spiritual heritage. That cosmic view encompasses preserving life for the sake of life. As a spiritual being you play many roles that you are not aware of. Usually, all you can see is the third-dimensional roles you assume, but in your dreams and outside of your physical awareness, you may be performing many tasks for the universe and for God.

Meditating and praying for a few minutes each day will begin to reestablish your awareness of your connection to your soul and God. Your ego may put up a ferocious struggle to put forth its agenda in your life. Your ego will tell you that you don't have time to pray, and maybe while reading this you heard a dozen excuses why you can't. Your soul will wait until you surrender, then drop a new blueprint into place. You will find your life's work when you're willing to give up your preconceived ideas as to what it ought to look like — and it can look like almost anything. You might be here to experience worldly goods and wealth. My friend was a gardener because his life purpose was to learn about the earth. You might be here to experience power or service; be a Bill Gates or a Bill Clinton; perhaps be a Mother Teresa, who lived without wealth. You will discover that your soul's blueprint will fit you perfectly. It will be custom-made for you, washed, pre-shrunk, pressed, and ready for you to wear out into the world.

The simple act of discovering your purpose and your unique capability to fulfill that purpose will do much to reestablish your connection with God and a realization of your own divinity. There is a still and silent place inside you, a peaceful place of immeasurable strength and resourcefulness. It is the neutral zone, free of judgment. There you will learn to find solace. It is from that place that you can create your heart's desire. You will know when you are doing the right thing because it will bring you joy and fulfillment — and as a creation of God, you deserve nothing less than unalloyed happiness.

Creativity

~ ~ ~ ~ ~ ~ ~ ~ ~ ~ ~ ~ ~ ~ ~

The heart of creativity is imagination. It is your imagination that connects you with all of creation and with the universal mind of creativity. Your individual creativity is simply an expression of the creative energy of the universe. It is through imagination that the world of form is created. You and I cannot see the subtle mystery of our thoughts and ideas taking form, but everything begins with imagination, visualization and thought. The pictures in your mind become the reality you play out. Nurturing your imagination is the first step toward restoring your creativity. You do that by acknowledging your imagination as the greatest gift from God, not by doubting it or trivializing it, but by believing in your imaginative abilities.

It is through the visual images held in your imagination that you begin to produce the changes you desire in your world. Your feeling nature propels the energy of creativity into the physical world, where it becomes the reality you witness. However, action is required, and for many, this is where things get sticky. Exactly what is the right thing to do often seems nebulous and obscure, but that confusion is simply a symptom of your ego's resistance to change. You'll find that your path of creativity, whether it be in the arts or any other field, is strewn with the road-blocks your personality creates. If this happens, do not criticize yourself. Growing beyond your past limitations is a gradual process. When you can lift yourself by your boot-straps, your action will move you forward.

If you've been stalled and inactive in your life for a considerable amount of time, inaction will become your reality and it will take conscious effort and action to regain the momentum lost during your inactive stage. This is because your personality, your ego, has become identified and polarized with inaction. As you rebuild your vision through imagination, your feelings begin to stir. As you begin to release them through action you build momentum toward change.

One morning, my friend Kay and I sat together drinking coffee and discussing our troubles finding creative outlets for our work. She had really just begun her explo-ration into her spirituality and her own creativity. I suggested we go to a nearby psychic fair going on that day to see if any of the practitioners there could shed some light on the issue of creativity. The psychic that Kay saw told her that the energy around her throat chakra was blocked.

The throat chakra is a subtle human energy system that controls creativity and expression. It isn't something that can be measured by modern science, but all the ancient wisdom of our history speaks of these energy systems. Anything that causes distortion or contraction of those subtle energies will limit expression. A lot of fear and anger can be held in those energy centers.

The psychic told Kay that her throat chakra was being blocked because she'd been raised in a family that didn't value creative expression. Kay began to explore her past and recalled that children were to be seen and not heard, and that girls were not allowed to express anger. Creative expression was simply frivolous behavior. When she went against that training, she was breaking one of those subconscious contracts she'd made with her family, and the fear of being punished for speaking out or expressing herself is what actually created the blocks. As she released those thinking patterns and restored her creativity, she discovered that she harbored latent talent for writing and painting.

Claudia had been a friend of mine for a long time. She was an attorney and I hired her to do some legal work for me that required a great deal of correspondence. As I read the many letters she wrote, it became clear to me that she had a real gift with words, one that was so obvious I envied her. When I shared with her my observation of her skill, she confided that she had a fantasy of writing fiction but didn't feel gifted enough to write for the public at large.

Claudia knew I was a counselor, so I suggested that she come to my office to see if there was something subconsciously holding her back, since her writing ability was certainly not the issue. Over several sessions it came out that Claudia's uncle was a very frustrated would-be writer, one who neglected his family for his aspired-to vocation. As a result of the rejections that he received from publishers, he began to drink until he was consumed by alcoholism. As a child, Claudia had heard of his fate countless times at the dinner table. Subconsciously she became convinced that writing and lack of responsibility went hand in hand. She had a family herself, and was determined not to follow in the footsteps of her berated uncle. Clearing this subconscious pattern allowed her to begin living her fantasy of writing, and at this time she is negotiating a contract with a publisher for her first book.

The polarity experienced in this case is action opposing inaction. The moment you decide to act, all forces geared toward inaction will rise. Fear and doubt will quickly surface. Your old programming, which got you stuck in the first place, will scream your unworthiness, lack of talent, and just plain foolishness. This always happens when you move from an old familiar paradigm into a new one. For many of you, your creative impulses will cycle. As you become sensitive to that cycle, you can use it to know when to rest and when to launch a new round of creativity. Nothing is more important to those who want to be creative than self-understanding. There is a time for planning and a time for action.

Inertia though, is not always the result of being stuck and afraid of change. Sometimes it can be a natural part of your cycle. You need to understand this because inaction isn't always the result of all the programs about your unworthiness, or all the doubts you have about your abilities. Inertia is the natural state of a polarized world and you will have to learn to cope with it in a positive way. This is not offered as an excuse, however, and you need to be able to see through the doubts your ego puts in front of you. If you are having doubts and not encountering actual roadblocks, then it is your ego and not naturally occurring inertia.

Recently, while I was thinking about holding a workshop in the area where I live, it was clear to me what to do and what to expect. During the middle of the night as

I was lying awake and thinking about my plans, I began to doubt. I could feel myself not wanting to proceed. Of course, my ego jumped in and did its very rational dance about why my plans were flawed, and brought up past mistakes. I felt as if something was trying to convince me not to move ahead. As soon as I realized this was my ego's fear speaking, I was able to move forward. You must learn to dissociate from, and step outside of, your ego's fearful, senseless chatter. The first thing to take note of when your ego starts shooting down your dreams is whether your thinking stems from the past. Is your focus upon past failures, mistakes you have made, and fear of the unknown? Are you hearing the voice of your parents, saying you'll never amount to anything, and that your ideas are all just foolishness? If so, then that's your ego talking, and, like a radio, just turn it off.

Children are the most naturally creative people. They have not learned that their creativity may be seen as foolishness. They see in their own creations the grandness of creativity, simply for the sake of creativity. Children are propelled into joy by the mere act of creating. God bless those parents who can nurture creativity. No doubt you collected the attitudes of your parents regarding your creative endeavors, whether they expressed them vocally or not. As a child, you pick up the subtle feelings and nuances that do not approve, and the effects of those attitudes are carried into adult life, appearing as your own worst critic, the tiny voice that never appreciates and always depreciates. Your job is to embrace those negative thoughts, understanding them for what they are, and then let them go and return to the action side of the action-inaction polarity.

I grew up with a young man who wanted to be a blacksmith. At the time, it appeared that there was no way in hell he could actualize his desire and make a living at it. That was before the historic preservation movement. Since then, his skill at fabricating and repairing wrought iron and creating decorative metal implements has been in great demand. I know that as a boy, he received a lot of criticism of his desire to become a blacksmith.

In much of society you are recognized as creative if you do something in art or music, and depending on whom you ask, sometimes writing is considered creative. Don't let your creativity be defined by cultural norms, by whether you can sculpt statues, paint, or do anything else that is commonly accepted as artistic. All of life is a creative expression, not just the arts. Helen Keller was deaf and blind almost from birth, yet she learned to write, read, and even speak. Could any of us hope to equal the creativity that it took her to surmount the obstacles she faced? Anyone who has raised a child is aware of the creativity it takes to raise children. And businesses large and small live and die by the creativity of the owners or managers. Marketing, advertising, programming, accounting — these are all creative expressions, although one hopes one's accountant doesn't become *too* creative.

Make no mistake about it, you are creative. Those who think they are not haven't yet allowed creativity's development, or they've been stifled as children. This is perhaps the single most debilitating thing that can happen to a child. Parents, adults, or peers are critical of a child's creativity, and eventually the child will lose the desire to be creative and risk disapproval of others. Unappreciative parents who can't acknowledge their children's creativity were most likely denied their own creative expression.

Generation after generation, the creativity of children is suppressed until only a few can express their creativity openly and without feeling guilty or threatened. And isn't it ironic that we as a society often revere great artists, but cannot acknowledge creativity in the most impressionable members of our society?

Creativity, imagination and visualization are functions of the right brain. Inner knowing, inspiration, psychic awareness, imagination, and visualization are right-hemisphere qualities. The right brain is the terrain of daydreaming, contemplation, prayer and meditation. We live in a left-brained, analytical society, and these qualities are highly valued and recognized. Society has become addicted to the analytical, scientific process since the beginning of the industrial revolution over three hundred years ago. Science is of course focused on the outer world, resolving problems with painstaking analysis. Science and law are two very left-brain fields, and both are exalted for their analytical nature. However, major break-throughs in science are always the result of intuition, precognition, flashes of insight, sudden awareness, or just plain inner knowing, all of which are right-brain qualities.

If you are strongly analytical and left-brained, you will probably have to nurture your connection to your right brain to bring forth your creativity. Balance of the left and right is easily accomplished through meditation. Sometimes very natural activities, such as driving down long lonely stretches of highway, will do that. For me, just driving down the freeway when traffic isn't too heavy will stimulate my intuition and creativity. I also use tarot cards. Sometimes the symbolism of a selected card stimulates my right brain. Your dreams are a function of your right hemisphere. Dreams are symbols designed to inform you of many things, including which course of action to pursue.

Whether or not you currently think of yourself as being creative, you can develop your creativity. A friend of mine did this by resurrecting a past life in which she was a painter. Interests and skills you have in this lifetime are often the result of a past life seeping through the veil of time. Could everyone do this? Probably, but they would first have to believe it is possible. If your belief system says no to past lives, or is skeptical, you can forget that avenue, but that avenue does exist. How do you think child prodigies acquire their skills? It takes more than natural ability to become a concert pianist by the age of ten or twelve, or sometimes even younger.

Creativity is a spiritual quality. It is divinely inspired. It is the core of your existence — not just your art or writing, but your very existence itself. Everyone is creative because, essentially, the universe, God, and your soul are creative. This universe is dynamic. It is constantly changing, shaping, and unfolding. You are a part of the whole creation, and you are constantly changing and being reborn at all levels. You are part of the creative process of the universe. You are creation and have come here to play your part in the unfolding of this universe. You can access your creativity no matter how deeply buried it is. If you draw a blank at this thought you probably have a lot of work to do, or at least a lot of introspection, meditation, and obstacle-clearing ahead. Your creativity is God's gift to you. Your gift to God is to be creative.

If you haven't been able to express yourself creatively either as a child or as an adult, it is the result of a blocked throat chakra. This subtle human energy center is the center of your creative expression. Blocked expression is an epidemic in our society, as children aren't allowed to express anger and other feelings. This is especially true for women. They are taught that to express anger is not ladylike, but women, of course, have anger just like men do. Expressing feelings and emotions is an essential part of being human, yet most people are afraid of expressing how they really feel at any given moment. The creative process is entirely one of expressing feelings and emotions. You remove blocks to your expression the same way you clear any other unwanted blockage: by introspection, by becoming aware of your underlying fears, and by releasing those worn-out psychological programs and beliefs that no longer serve you.

There are many other techniques for clearing blocked chakras. Throat chakras in particular are often blocked because you haven't expressed your anger, and so you will have to do that first. Try screaming profanities into a pillow for starters — without a pillow if your neighbors can take it. Most people are completely out of touch with their anger. They have stuffed it so deep, they do not even know they are angry.

The more connected you are to your energies, especially to your higher energies, the more creative you will be. Creativity is an experience of your higher nature being expressed through you. I have noticed that many teachers and creative people experience a shift to higher consciousness when they begin their work. This is a strong reinforcer of the benefits of doing meditation and clearing work. The more you do, the easier it is to shift to those higher levels when performing a creative endeavor.

As I said before, once you make a commitment to your creativity, your doubts will surface and tell you all manner of negative things. You will likely hear the negative voices of your parents, or perhaps simply feel their attitudes toward your creativity. Whatever their attitudes and beliefs were, you carry them in your energies and genes. What makes matters worse is that you are not only hearing the voices of your parents, but your grandparents and their parents as well. That might be the real reason for the development of your own creativity, to break the chain of that entire genetic program once and for all so future generations will be able to move into their creativity with ease. It is not well known what that comment from the Bible about the sins of the fathers being visited upon the sons really means, but it is clear to me what it has meant to my genetic chain. There are precious few creative people in my lineage.

Exploring your creativity is just one step. We continue referring to the neutral zone because you must also learn to step outside of polarity, or at least not become polarized by the negative side of every equation. As long as you have a need to know what the outcome of your actions will be, you are polarized, living without trust. I know that when I am writing, doubt will arise about my own abilities. My negative inner voice doesn't think there is a writer in me, or that anyone will be interested in what I have to say, but because I take my own advice seriously, I am able to keep on. So too must you persist. Perhaps no other quality will mean as much to your growth and creativity as will persistence. Remember, persistence is the carbon that will make you steel.

There is an addictive quality to being blocked. There certainly isn't any risk involved in wallowing in your inability to move through your blocks. You can use it to blame your parents or teachers for not recognizing your innate creativity, for not knowing who you are. Better still, you can find others to encourage your despair and anger at being slighted, being left out of the creative equation by God. Know that they may pity you, and even drink with you, but it will not help one iota. You will simply retreat further from the day your creativity will become a shining example for all to see.

The development and pursuit of creativity are essentially the same for everyone. With the exception of a select few, they require a lifetime of vigilance because real creativity doesn't have a term, it is never ending. Many artists have maintained and acquired their skills at the edge of a lifetime, doing their most creative work in their eighties and even nineties. Nourishing your creativity, whether in its infancy or far into your creative life, requires that you continuously monitor your thoughts for those old programs of lack and limitation that currently hold you in check and keep you from actualizing who you really are.

The polarized world has only two points of experience, fear or love. Creativity is most certainly an aspect of the latter. Love releases, allows, moves, creates; fear does exactly the opposite — sticks, binds, contracts, refuses to go forward. You cannot release your blocks by ignoring them or denying them by saying to yourself, "Oh well, that must not be for me anyway." You can, of course, use any excuse you like to sell out your life to the darkness of quiet despair, but that is not the warrior's way. The way of the warrior may be filled with pain, but he is always looking to move to higher ground, to find real meaning, and to find the promise of love, creativity, and fulfillment.

You know in your heart that your joy lies not in hiding in the corner, wallowing in self-deprecation and pity, but in moving through your inertia, doubt, and insecurities, despite what you have experienced as a child or as an adult. Your creative force is released by your courage, the courage to face the world and your inner demons, to take a stand, to explore the world on your own terms, no matter what you have experienced in the past. The past is just that — *passed*. Don't let the voices of the past hound you. Shake them off, put them behind you so they can no longer block you. It is by living in this moment that you allow your natural power and creativity to flourish.

8

Autonomy

~ ~ ~ ~ ~ ~ ~ ~ ~ ~ ~ ~ ~ ~ ~

There are some five billion people on this planet. Almost every one of them has accepted a very distorted version of reality, and done so without question. Most people believe that their lives are at the mercy of the actions of other people and a chaotic world. A majority of the planet's population lives in poverty, believing they are victims of circumstance. The truth is, every person is autonomous. This includes you. What does that mean? It means no outside authority can have any influence or effect on you, in any way whatsoever, unless you consent to it.

When I use the word autonomy in my conversations, I often get a rather confused look from those who hear it. I am not sure whether they do not understand the meaning of the word, or whether their reaction is the result of understanding the word, but never having thought of their lives in this context before. This is the definition provided for autonomous in my dictionary: *self-governing; independent; subject to its own laws only...* The idea of autonomy is indeed a radical concept for many, yet it is a central theme in all great spiritual teachings. You are the author of your life and no person or thing outside of yourself has anything to say or do about it. You make the choices. It is a one person show, and you are the only writer in the play that is your life.

Am I saying that no outside authority, person, group, or even institution has any authority over you unless you allow it? Yes, that's exactly what I'm saying. The belief that your world, the things you experience, the coincidences in your life and the people you meet are all the result of random chance is a great misunderstanding, although it certainly is convenient for those who want to pass the buck to others and continue to blame someone out there for their own lack and unhappiness. The buck stops right where you are, whether you choose to accept it or not.

Stress and anxiety are the result of believing that what you experience is out of your control, that you are a victim of chance and can be harmed by random events. The outer world is a reflection of your inner world and your beliefs. The beliefs you hold about yourself are "out-pictured" in your life. As a child, you automatically adopted the beliefs your parents put forth as their version of reality. You accepted their script for life as is. But chances are, your parents were very limited in their own understanding.

Most people do not easily accept the idea that they are totally responsible for everything that happens in their lives. For centuries, societies and cultures have gone to war, righteously blaming each other for their individual plights. Armies crossed boundaries to capture slaves and goods in order to improve their own lot, or as retaliation for wrong done to them. Today, helpless victims appear on the nightly news and talk shows with frightening regularity. The common denominator is that they are one and all the victims of random events that have no relationship to their own actions. It is understandable that the ordinary citizen doesn't accept his role on this drama. He has learned otherwise, and is constantly bombarded with statistics that support his fear. The truth is that you are created in the image of God. Why would God create you in his image and then leave you to wander the cosmos, a hapless victim of circumstances beyond your control? What a cruel fate that would be.

Your willingness to accept your autonomy, and therefore make it real, is somewhat dependent on the issues you came into this lifetime to experience. You are autonomous, but you do have a program, a very complex, dynamic, and unique program that your soul chose for you in this lifetime. It has certain restrictions and built-in boundaries. This is karma. It has been taught for centuries that this is absolute. Perhaps it was, but that is no longer the case. It is no longer absolute because of the current stage of evolution of the planet and humanity. If it is important for you to discover your own autonomy in this lifetime, you will likely find yourself polarized in the opposite belief of victimhood. The belief that outside forces have influence and even control over you. If you have been in denial of your autonomy for many lifetimes, purging that belief may be difficult but the rewards will be great. Those who are unwilling to look at their issues will find it very difficult to break those restrictive qualities of their blueprint. Awareness and understanding of the content of your blueprint are what allow you to transcend it.

We have discussed at length your ego's unwillingness to change. In general, it is only because of the pain in their lives that people finally become willing and motivated to change. This is unfortunate, but true. The truth is sought only after the life based on lies becomes unbearable. In and of itself your ego has no real power. It is like the autopilot on an airplane, following a computer that your parents and past programmed for you. Your beliefs provide the parameters of the flight program. It is very mechanical in its selection, following old beliefs without one iota of creativity or imagination. This is not bad, because once your beliefs are in alignment with universal principles — once they've been reprogrammed — you will never have to give them another thought.

This is how being autonomous can be your greatest strength. When you realize you are autonomous, you can create your life the way you want it, moment by moment, totally unconcerned by the outside world. You can, of course, choose to continue to act out your life as though others have authority over you, and you might have limited material success doing so. Yet the appearance that there is anyone else dictating what transpires upon the stage of your life is a great illusion. It is pure and simple illusion that anyone out there can make you happy or unhappy. You may have given them roles in your play, but you can hand them a different script any time you choose. You created all the characters you see. You hired the cast, you gave them their parts. Like all good actors, they are giving convincing performances. This analogy may seem quaint, even trite, to you, because it's too simple. "All I have to do is rewrite the script, and voila! Life will be a bowl of cherries?" Believe it or not, it could work as easily as that. You could simply surrender to the truth and rewrite your script. Or, like me, you may have to spend a decade or two reading everything in sight, looking for that magic bullet. The sooner you accept the responsibility for your script, the easier it will be for you to rewrite it. Once you say, "Yes, I have created that," you can then say, "Now I will create this."

The closest you come to an indelible script that cannot be changed is your karmic imprint, or blueprint. Cause and effect is a real phenomenon, but the opposite of that is a perfect state of grace that is neutral. You can erase and balance your karma and live from that state of grace in which there are no polarities. If you have studied ancient texts, you may have read that you are going to have a difficult time getting to this space. You won't. You may have been accumulating karma for 10,000 lifetimes, but that does not matter. The limitation of karma can be released with ease. The problem is that you are dealing with issues you aren't consciously aware of. You can erase your issues by becoming aware of them. Parts of your imprint pertain to this lifetime and other parts are relative to past lifetimes. Through an ancient mantra that uses the energy of your eighth chakra I have developed a process to induce memory and awareness of your subconscious mind. The process will release those people from your life who do not fit your new script. Of course, there are many other processes as well.

Roberta took seriously the challenge of rewriting the script for her life. She began a daily routine of affirmation. She wrote about loving, accepting parents, which hers were not. She wrote about all the love and acceptance surrounding her in her own life, which was not there when she began writing. After a few weeks of writing and dialoguing on paper about her ideal life, her life began to shift, ever so slightly. When she felt emotions in conflict with what she wrote, she allowed those feelings to emerge and cried or did whatever her feelings begged. Her life continued its gradual change for the better. She called me recently to tell me about the wonderful new man she was with and her great new job.

When you accept your autonomy, you are immediately confronted with the possibility that you are all things, that you are pure potential. It is this fact that you are autonomous that enables you to transcend your current limitations. You have chosen to read this book. Undoubtedly, this is not the result of ego's prodding, but of the urging of your soul, your inner light, because it is time for you to embrace a different perspective than the one your parents and other teachers in your life have bestowed upon you.

We have reached the absolute outer reaches of a great cosmic cycle. As we move back toward the center from which we came, it becomes easier to relinquish those erroneous belief systems. We all have the ability to go inward, and within we all have accurate compasses. You are indeed a spiritual being with unlimited potential, exploring a world of polarity and limitations, but that doesn't mean you have lost your ability to discern truth. In fact, you cannot lose anything because you are indeed autonomous and carry in your fields all the knowledge, information, and potential of a living God.

Within your energy capsule is a full complement of angels, guides, and masters. These higher beings you normally would see as something other than yourself, but they are not. These beings are higher aspects of yourself. They are what you are becoming, they are you. You have been taught that they are out there, separate from you. This is the height of man's ignorance and arrogance, the belief that you are separate from God. You could not be, even if that was what you truly desired.

Like Adam and Eve, we have eaten the forbidden fruit. Long ago in human history we left the neutral zone and began to view the world with our polarized belief in good and evil. The moment we left paradise and fell from grace was the same moment we attached the idea of "good" to one thing, and "bad"to another. This created something to fear. The rest is history, as we shall see.

Your autonomy, your state of grace, lies in how you choose to think. No matter what conditions exist in your life, what actions occur outside of your self, you choose how you will think about them. You can see yourself as the poverty-stricken victim of a sick society or as a child of God, blessed with the opportunity to rise above all adversity. You can see your journey as toil or as an effortless return to a consciousness of grace, as God designed. No matter who you are or where you have been in this lifetime or any other, you can literally change your mind and begin anew. Surviving your life is simply stepping into harmony with the universe, being in that place outside of polarity and duality where grace resides, the neutral zone. The universe did not make life difficult and painful, humankind did that on its own, and did a great job of it.You have been given the gift of choice. You can do nearly anything you can imagine yourself doing. Your imagination is there for you to use. Your creativity is there for you to use. And your hands were given to you so that you could shape your existence.

It is entirely up to you what you believe, whether to be hapless victim or creative powerhouse. But be sure that whatever you choose to believe about yourself will be actualized in your life. For better or for worse you chose the content of this lifetime, but because you are not eternally bound by karma, you can make and shape your experience any way you want to. You are the one who chooses to be beggar, sinner, or saint. In truth, you are autonomous, and you have potentials that rival those of the gods. It is up to you to decide the manner in which you develop and actualize your potential. There is simply no one calling the shots but you.

Being autonomous is an awesome responsibility. If you are ready to accept that much responsibility, you will begin to accelerate along a path of evolution. There really isn't anything to hold you back, except yourself.

9

Relationships

~ ~ ~ ~ ~ ~ ~ ~ ~ ~ ~ ~ ~ ~ ~ ~

Every relationship in your life is colored by the single most important relationship you have — your relationship with God. For most people that relationship creates the most significant polarity of all, namely, the belief that you and God are apart from each other. You cannot possibly feel secure when you believe that you are separate from the source of your consciousness, which is out there somewhere and far removed from you, untouchable. This is the source of primal pain and fear. It is the greatest anxiety of humankind, and it is why life appears to be so threatening.

Life itself poses no threat. Any threat is simply a magnification of your belief that you are separate from God. You search in many ways to reconnect with this foundation. All of your striving is trying to connect with the whole, the Source. You think a larger home, more money in your bank account, or a new car will make you more secure. But you have found the ego's appetite for such possessions to be insatiable.

Could an infant be satisfied if it could not find its mother's bosom? All of our political and religious structures, and even our corporations are an attempt at bridging the distance we perceive between ourselves and God. Throughout history there have been great teachings that have attempted to explain this and illustrate the oneness of creation, but few have taken them seriously. Mythology, ritual and symbolism are all attempts to increase our understanding of our relationship with God, and yet the masses remain confused and insecure in their knowledge of their true nature.

In order to change your relationship with God, your own self, and other people, you have to acknowledge the problem. You have to see the big picture and look for a way to heal the primary relationship that is your connection to every other thing. This certainly is no small task in a culture that to a large extent hides from, ignores, and even denies its own divinity. Denying who you are immediately blunts any attempt to rectify the problem. Religions and others who claim to have direct contact with God purposely keep others from a personal relationship with God. This is a convenient way for those who see themselves as ordained or having special privileges to make the case that ordinary people have no such rights in this manner. For centuries, those who tried to bypass the church and create an open door to God have been persecuted by the high priests of organized religion. Of course, the collective psyche maintains this memory and is deterred by it, albeit not consciously.

It is your relationship with God that sets the stage for all of your other relationships. God is your creator. Many therapists believe that no other issue really matters, and that restoring your connection with God and realizing who you truly are will heal all other issues. While this is fundamentally true, most people will benefit by taking smaller steps first. Healing the separation between you and God is the goal, but you will probably have to start with more peripheral issues like healing your relationship with your parents, spouse, children and others. All these issues are a warm-up, preparation for healing the biggest wound there is — your belief in separation between you and God.

Your biological parents are merely caretakers for this lifetime. You may have had hundreds, even thousands of biological caretakers throughout your soul's existence. Every incarnation puts you together with a new set of biological parents. However, souls do tend to reincarnate within the same grouping. There was a classic example of this with a group of people in a small town in Nevada that had memories of living together in the South during the Civil War. Many of these people appeared on local and national television, and the evidence they presented was very credible. No doubt you have been with your parents before. You, in your wisdom, selected the parents who would best facilitate the experiences you needed in this lifetime to balance your karma.

By being centered and listening from the neutral zone, you can experience what your soul and God desire for you. When you understand that the life you're experiencing is completely of your own choosing, there is often confusion and bewilderment. After all, if this is true, why would anyone choose a lifetime of such frequent and intense pain? If life truly was your choice, certainly you would have chosen something else. Many a sage has tried to explain the possible reasoning behind choices we make that do not appear "good." We make them to balance karma, to experience duality, and to find out who we are, as well as who we are not. On the surface it may appear as though you've made some kind of a mistake by picking a lifetime as difficult as this one has become, but your search for a solution brought you to this material, and to other resources which increase your understanding. It is virtually impossible for you to see the bigger picture as long as you are in a physical body and separated from knowing the wisdom of your soul's choices in this matter.

Think of it this way. A great eagle (your soul) drops a man (your physical body) in the middle of a great and tangled forest, which he is forced to hack his way through. While he struggles, he cannot understand why the eagle dropped him here in this wretched forest. But what he doesn't know, and the eagle does, is that just ahead is a lake and the man will be able to make a raft out of the wood he is cutting down.

To survive this reality with ease, you must learn to live without being polarized. You must be in that place of neutrality where there are no opposites, that place where God is still with you, and you are not alone, where there is no separation from the wisdom and joy of your higher nature. God and the self are one. The self is a graduation of the Creator — a lower frequency, yet the same intelligence.

Depending on where you are today, starting your relationship with God or reviewing it may be as simple as beginning to pray or meditate. It will most likely entail an exploration of your issues. As you explore, you begin to loosen the denial that creates the disconnection between you and God. Many people find this step of facing issues to be the most difficult, for reasons that never really make sense.

Mostly the great initial resistance is out of deference to your elders. It's another of those family contracts, because in a sense you have formed a pact with your parents to keep them from being exposed. For the good of the family you cannot completely accept that your parents were wrong. Honoring this deception has kept humanity bound to the wheel of pain and suffering for centuries. The truth will set you and every member of your family free, especially the generation to come, but also those who have already passed on.

I spent many years in psychoanalysis and participated in most modalities of self-exploration to one degree or another. They are all useful, but they are bandages, and most disguise the real problem. My psychoanalyst was the first person to discuss spiritual matters with me. He realized that ultimately we all have to embrace our spirituality if we are to survive and prosper here on Earth. Without under-standing the nature of your spiritual reality, you will always feel lost and abandoned, isolated and alone, angry and fearful. As long as your spirituality is not properly nourished, you will feel an emptiness inside.

An entire industry has grown up around counseling. Many therapies are aimed at teaching you how to deal with physical reality, to assist you in making better decisions in your life. Any therapy that increases your spiritual awareness can potentially repair the rift between you and God. There are many skills you can learn that can be useful in assisting you through some of the pitfalls you experience in your relationships. The awareness created by exploring your psyche will gradually allow the light of truth into the deepest crannies of your mind, and begin to restore your primary relationship with God.

The thing that keeps you from hearing the messages God sends to you is the same thing that diminishes your ability to listen to other people. People love good listeners, those who don't tune you out, just waiting for the chance to tell you about their own personal dramas. Most people are not good listeners because their own issues rise to the surface as soon as you begin to speak to them. It is impossible for you to be a good listener if your own psyche is a garbage can full of old fear and anger.

To listen, simply and really listen, is the greatest service you can offer others. Listen to them and hear what they say. And that is all God requests of you, that you listen to them. You cannot receive from him if you don't listen. You serve God by listening, and then it becomes clear what God would like you to do. An added benefit of listening is clarity around your own issues. That person in your life telling you all about her problems is alerting you to your own issues. The likelihood that she is in your life, yet you do not share similar issues, is nil. She is in your life because you share a similar pathology. She is there as an outer reflection of an inner condition.

Perhaps the most confusion we all face on this planet is the confusion and judgment around sexuality. To most people sex does not seem very godly or spiritual. The idea that some things are godly and some are not is simply another polarity. God doesn't make judgments about sexuality or anything else. Obviously, sexuality is God-given. Who do you think created sexuality? We are often taught that sex is not love. That simply is not true, except when it is sought out of fear, or a feeling of incompleteness. Sexual union is perhaps one of the few times we actually feel connected to someone else. This creates another paradox: The more disconnected you are from God and yourself, the less connected you can be with anyone else, sexually or otherwise.

Sex is really just another human experience. Neither the religious right nor the liberal left really understands human sexuality. The right obviously thinks it knows what is right and wrong for every individual under any circumstance, but its ignorance is plain to see. Only you can really determine what is right or wrong for you. Those who think they have the answers to these questions are simply deceiving themselves, and allowing others to decide for them.

I do believe you should honor any relationship agreements you make, but above all you should cease judgment of others. Of course, that is the hardest of all to do. Maybe it cannot be done in a human body, but certainly we can do a better job than we have been. Isn't it interesting that communication and sexuality are the two most important qualities of being human, yet are probably the most confused and distorted of all human characteristics in terms of our demonstrated understanding of them?

There are many issues that can separate you from God, but that separation will not be God's choice. If you see God as a vengeful, judgmental God you will want to hide your issues, suppress them. In the first place, you cannot hide anything from God. You are completely transparent in God's eyes. Secondly, the view that God is a vengeful, judgmental being is the result of our projecting human qualities onto God. It simply is not that way at all. Remember, we are created in God's image, not the other way around. God is love. Judgment is based in fear. It simply does not exist in the higher realms. Judgment is strictly a human experience. You must stop judging yourself; then you will not feel compelled to judge others.

Healing your issues with God can be as simple a process as praying. Prayer can be a wonderful means of communicating with and reconnecting to God. Pray during quiet times, and know that you are being listened to. Don't be afraid to express your feelings, your anger and your fear. The trick is to express these emotions, and then release them. You will receive assistance once you've cleared the path of your own fears and worries. Expressing your desire to heal will quickly draw to you what you need. Typically you will be led to some action you need to take.

When you pray, you'll want to watch out for a couple of minor things that can trip you up. First of all, do not start your prayer by stating what you want. It is far better to begin prayer with a statement of gratitude. You can ask for assistance and clarity, but stay away from statements that are negative, or express lack. Frequently such statements will be self-affirming anyway. For instance, the statements "God, I am always broke. I never have enough. I need more," will simply perpetuate your limitation. The word *want* is self-affirming. Express gratitude for what you do have and pray for the wisdom and clarity to recognize the support the universe will offer you. And do so knowing that you will receive that support.

Separation from God is the cause of many, if not all of the difficulties in your life. It is the primary cause of the deep feelings of abandonment and anger. Intellectually, you may be thinking that you know God didn't abandon you, but your feelings may be saying something else. Working with clients tells me that you are very likely in denial of your anger toward God for abandoning you. Why do so many people deny their anger with God? Because religions teach that God holds grudges and believes in retribution. Those are, again, human qualities that have been erroneously projected onto God. Still, we would rather not voice our frustration, just in case.

The first time I mentioned to Susan that most people are deeply angry with God and feel abandoned by their creator, she vehemently stated that she knew God had not abandoned her. However, her response seemed very mental and intellectual, without a lot of real feeling behind her words. Then one day during a session with me, she became aware of her own anger toward God for abandoning her. That revelation brought about an eruption of painful feelings which lasted an hour the first time they surfaced. Then a seemingly strange thing happened in her relationship with her mate. She grew closer to him and their level of communication deepened. This was a result of her healing her relationship with God, and therefore with her own self. Instead of harboring thoughts of separating herself from her current relationship, she began to consciously create the change she desired by settling differences with love rather than anger, control and conflict.

Life is a path of self-discovery. That self-discovery will eventually lead you back home to an understanding of who you are. Certainly the day will come when, through revelation or other means, your awareness expands into total recall of your own divinity and you heal all the issues of this lifetime and others. You will then return to your natural state of grace, wisdom, and love. You will no longer bear the ignorance of a disconnection from God as you do now. Because you live in a polarized, linear world, you may have to make this journey one step at a time. But even that isn't all bad. The lessons learned one step at a time will certainly never be forgotten, and you will have no need to repeat them in the future.

10

Talking With God

~ ~ ~ ~ ~ ~ ~ ~ ~ ~ ~ ~ ~ ~ ~ ~

There is a divine plan for this planet. Since you are here you're a part of that plan. Your very existence is proof of your participation in this immaculate scheme. Most people have given little thought to why they are here. The business of everyday life seems overwhelming most of the time, and you haven't been taught the art of listening to the myriad ways God speaks to you. While the Judeo-Christian tradition stresses the necessity of daily intimate communication with God, it doesn't believe in every individual's ability to receive the constant wisdom flooding through our perceptual systems. In fact, for the past 2,000 years churches and institutions have supported, encouraged, and even demanded that you turn to them for spiritual guidance, persecuting those who refused to do so. As a result, that memory of religious persecution has become part of the race memory of this planet. Therefore, you may initially experience fear when you consider eliminating the middle man and restoring your own individual connection with God.

There are many levels of communication with higher sources; you can connect with your soul and higher self, your angels, guides, archangels, and even God. After all, these are all individualized aspects of God. Each level in ascension is a higher, finer frequency than the others, God being the highest yet most subtle of them all. Of course God can speak to you directly using any means imaginable. Some people find it easier to communicate with their own higher selves, or their angels and guides, before approaching God. Wherever you seek guidance, you can be sure there are higher beings eagerly awaiting your effort at communication.

Your body and your feelings can be compared to an antenna that connects this physical reality to your soul and spirit. Learning to recognize the guidance that is always there for you is no more difficult than changing the channels on your television set. Yet many of you who read this will be confused as to precisely how to do this. You don't need to take any classes or attend workshops. Those extracurricular activities may speed the process, but they aren't mandatory.

In the late 1980s the channeling of spiritual information became an international phenomenon, although there have always been channelers or mediums. Speaking tongues, which is mentioned in the Bible, is a type of channeling. To me it was something new and exciting. A channel, as it was called at the time, was portrayed mostly as a mere parlor game. However, the experience of channeling is valid and quite real, and it in fact cultivates a more intimate relationship with the higher realms, and eventually with God. The amount of spiritual information that has

come through channels in the past century is literally
changing the mind of man. Still, channeled information is
like all other input in that you must choose what you will
accept as real, and what you will refuse. That something is
being channeled does not necessarily mean it is true, or
even true for you, and you must decide for yourself what
will be your truth.

You need to know this because of the fact that not all
beings are from the higher realms. The Bible speaks of this
and warns you to make sure that the being you are communicating with is from the level of Christ. "Beloved, believe
not every spirit, but test the spirits whether they are of God;
because many false prophets are gone out into the world.
Hereby know ye the Spirit of God: Every spirit that confesseth that Jesus Christ is come in the flesh is of God; and
every spirit that confesseth not that Jesus Christ is come in
the flesh is not of God." (1 John 4:1-3). This is why it is so
important for you to decide what is true and what is not. It's
also another reason why you should seek professional
training in how to channel.

I first learned the skill of channeling in a class with
sixty other people in Northern California in the late eighties.
During those early classes it certainly never occurred to me
that some time in the future God would actually speak to
me, and even through me. It seemed altogether too fantastic.
The first being who spoke through me called himself Joseph
and was from the angelic realm. One of the first things he
talked about was my writing. He told me I would write three
books. The first one would be about some esoteric information that had not come to the planet before then. That was
my first book, *Creating Your Light Body*.

Over the next couple of years I refined my skills and
began to bring through a lot of psychic information for those

who came to me. One lady wanted to know where to move to. Through channeling, she was advised that her first choice would be very dangerous for her. She decided to accept that information as truth and didn't move there. Subsequently, there was a devastating earthquake in that area.

After taking countless classes and becoming well versed and proficient in channeling, I began teaching others how to become channels for their own angels and guides. I began to realize that channeling was a very useful skill in many ways because it taught people how to sense and feel very subtle energies, energies as subtle as the energies of creation, and their own auras. The ability to sense subtle energies can be used to great advantage in a person's growth and healing. The beings, angels and others, that are typically channeled are very high in vibration. Everything is energy, and the universe uses high-level energies to heal and to communicate with people.

When teaching channeling, I use a number of techniques to teach people how to feel and access those higher energies. There are many ancient tools for working with subtle energies, especially mantras. My book *Ancient Wisdom* has an entire process for doing this. I place people in a trance or hypnotic state when teaching them to channel, and work directly with their higher nature, which has an innate ability to work with subtle energy. At that point I simply lead them through the experience. People are almost always successful on the first attempt, but it is a skill and it takes practice to develop a high level of ability.

Another positive benefit of channeling is the immense sense of support it instills. Everyone needs support, physically, emotionally and spiritually. The hosts of heaven can support you perfectly on many levels. The reason it is hard for you to hear, sense, or feel those beings is your belief that you only have five senses. That simply is not so. You have the capacity, especially through your feelings, to perceive the communication of those beings who wish to speak to you. With training and practice, you can greatly enhance your skills at communing with them. The information God sends to you moment by moment will have a hard time getting through to you if you are not in touch with your feelings. It's like flying in a fog without instruments. Would you board a jumbo jet or any other plane with its guidance system disconnected? Of course not.

Karen found that God was speaking to her all the time. She was an avid gardener and raised many different types of flowers. She was aware that even under the best of circumstances, some of the flowers she planted would do very well while others died. Roses were her favorite and symbolized love and compassion for her. Without actually realizing it she had become contracted in her relationship with her mother. At the same time that there was an infestation of aphids attacking her roses, her mother became seriously ill. As those two seemingly unconnected events occurred in her life she felt powerless against them, and it did not register with her that the cause of either event had anything to do with her.

One day, in meditation, Karen saw a picture of her entire garden falling into complete decay. She was too insightful to miss that warning. As she began to contemplate what that vision meant, she realized it was a reflection of her struggle with her mother. It was at that point that she decided to forgive herself and her mother, and accept life as it was. Within a matter of only a few days, her mother and her flower garden began to recover simultaneously.

In Kansas City, I was trying to locate a site for a new branch of the carpet cleaning business I owned, but I had an unusually difficult time finding a suitable place. It was taking months when usually it took just a few days. I didn't realize it at the time, but the difficulty we were having finding a space to rent was an indicator of things to come. Kansas City became a very difficult place for my business to be successful. Had I been more observant at the time, I would have recognized the trouble we had settling there as a sign.

It is vital to your survival that you strengthen your awareness in listening for God's messages. We have suggested that God speaks to you in certain ways, but you may have a different way of receiving information that is completely unique to who you are. It is important that you determine what that is for you, and then nurture that connection. Receiving messages in one form or another, whether from God or your own intuition, cuts the work of surviving your life in half. It is a major step toward a life lived with ease, in the neutral zone.

Everything in your world is connected in one way or another. We are all plugged into the circuits that carry a current of messages from the universe, but in most cases the switch is turned off. Your belief in the separation between you and everything else fosters the appearance of being cut off from all that support and information. But when you are consciously connected to the universe and can respond to divine guidance, you automatically become a co-creative human. You are then working hand in hand with God to create heaven on earth. Imagine living a life without doubt and fear, in which you are directly guided by angels and God. Such a life is possible, but first you must develop your senses. The place to start is simply to acknowledge the truth of what you have just read. Accept that you are not separate from God, and believe that a purely joyous and fulfilling life is possible.

The second step is to dissociate from polarity and move into the neutral zone. Refuse the polarity of separation which states that you and God are separate and disconnected from each other, that God is in heaven and you are here on Earth, which probably feels more like hell sometimes. It has been said thousands of times before that you and the Creator are one, but this is not easily understood or experienced when you are polarized. Your connection with God can be restored easily, but it requires effort and focus on your part. You will have to take some time to develop your ability to perceive beyond your five senses. This ability is innate in human beings, although for centuries it has lain mostly dormant. Throughout history there have been individuals who have kept the memory of the senses beyond the physical five alive for all of us. They have kept the doorway open through which we can all experience and communicate with God.

The outer world is symbolic. You can learn to see guidance in all of your experiences, whether it is something you see in a public park that triggers the thought and understanding of something else, or a sentence overheard while flipping channels on the television that pertains exactly to what you were wondering about; the universe has a message for you. All of the events in your life can tell you a lot about what is going on in your psyche. Being stuck in traffic while going to work might suggest that it's time to consider changing jobs. A traffic jam may seem too commonplace to attach any symbolism to it, but again we say: Withholding nothing, the universe is symbolic. You are probably unfamiliar with the language of symbolism, but this language surrounds you, and you can benefit greatly from learning to listen to the universe speak to you through everything.

During the quiet times of contemplation and meditation, God can most easily speak to you. Your job is simply to provide the time and space for this to happen. The phone is already ringing, you just have to take the time to pick it up. This will enable you not only to survive your life, but to completely fulfill your purpose on this planet as well. While in meditation, periods of deep contemplation, or even altered states such as dreaming and daydreaming, your brain functions on alpha brain waves. As your brain waves slow, you become open to other dimensions of awareness. Such altered states of consciousness are associated with higher states of consciousness. Your solar plexus and heart center are another direct connection to the universe. Everyone has felt a clenched fist in the solar plexus as that nerve center warns you of an impending problem, or even a catastrophic event. That is but one example of God speaking to you through your feelings and your nervous system. There is always a broadcast coming to you through your feelings.

The universe provides constant signposts and messengers. Your thoughts are another way the universe communicates with you, but it is a little trickier to distinguish God's voice from the chatter of your own mind. The test is whether the messages are positive or negative, whether based in fear or love. In order to be sure, test them against how they feel to you. Anyone familiar with his chakra system knows that positive feelings emanate from the heart chakra and negative feelings from the solar plexus, where the third chakra is located. Your intuition is another way God speaks to you. The hard part for most people isn't being able to feel their intuition, but to trust those feelings.

You are an integral part of the flow of energy and information between God and earth. You're constantly relaying the energy of God, which actually nourishes the planet. Therefore you have the role of interpreter and mediator for God. Even if you wanted to, you couldn't remove yourself from that stream of information. The point is that at any given moment you are receiving enough information to insure your survival physically, emotionally, spiritually, and financially.

Another way God speaks to you is through others. This is probably one of the hardest lessons to learn: Those who you are least likely to listen to can sometimes bring you the most important messages. Likewise, a complete stranger may appear and speak to you of something very important. It's all too easy to discount the messages of a complete stranger. Loved ones and complete strangers are the people you are least likely to listen to, yet they can be your greatest resource. The feedback you get from those close to you is immeasurable and invaluable. Potentially, they are your greatest teachers.

The universe is alive with angelic presence, guides, masters, and devas whose sole function is to help you through your life. There is literally a host of ascended beings such as Jesus, the archangels Gabriel, Michael, and Raphael, and others of equal stature who are standing by to communicate with you and assist you with your soul's plan for your life. Every person alive has guardian angels who guide and assist them, who are with them from birth. Yet few people hear anything other than the monkey-like chatter of their own minds. Your ego is not a guidance system. The partnership of co-creation you exist within is not between you and your ego. True co-creation is a partnership between you and God.

You may decide for yourself that you have an affinity for angels or guides, or even the devic kingdom. This may be the result of past-life experiences, or even *having once been an angel yourself*. There are many angels who have decided to incarnate as humans today for one reason or another. There are healers worldwide who speak the devic language. On a recent visit with a renowned healer in Thailand, a group of us were taught how to use the devic language. This is an ancient tradition and has aided the healing of illnesses in Thailand for centuries. This, of course, would seem ludicrous to western physicians. However, in Thailand it is used singularly or with other techniques to routinely perform what would be considered miracles.

Devic language is not used in the sense that words are manipulated to convey your thoughts linguistically. Rather, you allow a higher consciousness to come through you tonally. You become a channel for the master devas who work with your personal devas, who provide the communication and adhesion your physical body needs to function. Working in this way to help others heal disease is truly a rewarding and co-creative experience.

Consciousness itself is unbounded by human limitations and beliefs about consciousness. It matters little to the devic kingdom, angels or guides what the beliefs of humanity are regarding their existence. The moment you are willing to call upon them, they stand ready to serve as intermediaries between you and God. Pure consciousness is God. When it comes cloaked as the consciousness of a specific thing, or place, it is only because an aspect of God has taken on a specific role to assist its own evolution and unfolding.

Your journey here on earth can become a co-creative experience, with the universe guiding you through what was once the minefield of your life. This idea of living life effortlessly doesn't mean that you won't take actions or make choices. Effortlessness implies that you will never again doubt your choices, or fear the consequences of your actions. Once you begin to perceive the symbolism surrounding you — which is God talking to you — then there will be light on your path, and your way will be made clear.

Your job is to learn to listen.

11

The Mouth Of God

~ ~ ~ ~ ~ ~ ~ ~ ~ ~ ~ ~ ~ ~ ~

The mouth of God is a metaphor for a chakra or energy system that sits at the base of the head, at the precise location of the medulla oblongata. It is the most important energy center humans have. Unlike all of your other chakras, the mouth of God is unique because it has only one function: the induction of higher level spiritual energies, those of a much higher frequency than what is normally thought of as human. That aspect of your energies we call soul is manifested on higher levels of consciousness. In the metaphysical realm, those higher energies are said to be on a higher dimension. Many would say those higher energies exist upon the fourth, fifth, six, seventh, and higher dimensions. The energy center known as the mouth of God can actually transcend all of those levels and connect you to the Source.

Because of this singular function, the mouth of God is your main connection with energies of a spiritual nature. It is the main access point for your higher self, the angels, devas, and masters of the higher realms. That there is such a center in the human energy field is wonderful news to many. However, before you begin to celebrate, know that for most this chakra is but a pinhole, and all but a tiny portion of those energies never reaches the average human.

Energies on this physical dimension of ours are ordinarily much lower and slower. To raise consciousness it is necessary to balance, harmonize, and raise the frequencies of the human energy system. Every spiritual process is an attempt to do exactly that, from clearing chakras, to raising kundalini, to clearing the emotional body, to activating the mouth of God. Of course, some processes are more efficient than others, and the mouth of God is the most efficient process I have experienced.

At this time there are many techniques emerging that are designed to assist the spiritual seeker in his or her quest. You must be very discerning because many of these processes do not live up to their billing. The reason for this is that many teachers are working at the astral level, below the fourth dimension, and they are not aware of it. They believe they are connected to much higher levels, but most are not. Teachers cannot take you where they have never been themselves.

Once the mouth of God is activated, it begins to clear your chakra system of lower energies, fear, and other debris. The purging of your chakras is of primary importance to your growth, especially that of the lower three chakras. As you clear the lower chakras, that energy moves upward and fuels the heart center. The lower chakras then also come under the influence of the heart chakra. In time there is a unifying of all the chakras with the heart. It has been said that at some point in your evolution there will be only one chakra, the heart center. All will become unified with the heart.

The heart center contains the essence of God and is in charge of healing, love, compassion, forgiveness, gratitude, wisdom and understanding. The wisdom self is contained in the heart and is the seat of all understanding. The heart is feminine and is the receptor for love and abundance.

When the mouth of God is activated, it floods the heart center with higher energies and raises the energy of your heart center. The heart center is not located at the physical heart, but at the thymus area. The chakras in the upper body — the heart, the throat chakra, the third eye, (or Asna center, which is located just above the eyebrows in the center of the forehead), and the crown at the top of the head — are all of a higher, finer vibration, have to do with your spirituality, and are greatly influenced by the mouth of God. The throat is located just below the mouth of God and is flooded with higher energies as it is opened. You may find that you cannot help but express yourself and your creativity once your mouth of God is opened. The third eye, crown, and medulla form a triangle when the mouth of God is activated. The triangle is the universal symbol of power. The third eye gives you sight, knowledge, intuition, and connection beyond time and space. The crown is the center of your mastery and enlightenment. As the mouth of God is activated, you become a force for change, not only of the self, but of the planet.

All who become activated reach out to every other person on the planet and begin to facilitate their enlightenment and activation as well as their own. At some point, critical mass will activate everyone upon the earth and it will become a planet of enlightened beings. In the meantime, it is up to each and every one of us to do our part to speed up the process.

My own activation has created a subtle and not so subtle enhancement of many spiritual qualities. It brought my higher self into my awareness and energies, and greatly enhanced my creativity, intuition, inner knowing, wisdom and understanding, connecting me with my Christ self.

I arrived late in the afternoon at the Albuquerque airport and was picked up by a friend of Lorenzo's, who, like Lorenzo, lived in Magdelina, which was more than a hundred mile ride through the desert. The first thing you think of when you arrive in Magdelina is whether anyone really lives there. I didn't count the houses but there looked to be no more than fifty, and most didn't seem occupied. A gas station, a grocery store, a small hardware store and a sleepy dry goods store served the people in a fifty-mile radius. I'd planned to spend my spare time meditating, which was fortunate because there wasn't anything else to do. Magdelina had obviously been a thriving mining town, but the mines had petered out long ago and the town had gone downhill ever since.

Lorenzo lived in a cabin at the edge of town in the middle of a ten-acre patch of desert with no shade from trees or anything else. He spent most of his time in meditation beneath a large ceiling fan and seemed totally oblivious to his surroundings.

I was prepared to spend two weeks with Lorenzo learning the secret mantras, mudras and invocations that activate the mouth of God. There were two of us who'd arrived to take the training and each of us was assigned a little brick cabin next to our host's dwelling. Lorenzo had told me over the phone that the first activation would be done shortly after our arrival. He was a stout powerful-looking man with a paunch from sitting too much and not getting enough exercise. He had the eyes and expression of a wise owl who knows the location of a secret cache of mice, while all the other owls are still hunting the forest. He obviously didn't like to shave, and sported one of the bushiest beards I had ever seen.

Before becoming enlightened he was an art director for a Madison Avenue advertising firm. He didn't speak much except when he was teaching. Casual conversation seemed to be something he left behind when he migrated to New Mexico.

I knew that a mouth of God activation was done in three half-hour sessions, sometimes a little longer, during which time Lorenzo spoke the prayers and invocations, and performed the mudras associated with activating the mouth of God. Occasionally I heard the words and felt his touch. Although I knew the mouth-of-God activation was something that can be done in groups, or over the phone, I had chosen to appear in person.

As I sat listening to Lorenzo speak, I moved in and out of conscious awareness of what was going on. I experienced a tremendous influx of energy at the back of my head where the medulla is located, and my third eye, the chakra in the middle of the forehead between the eyebrows, began to pulse. This third eye is a tunnel to psychic awareness and gives you the ability to see into the future.

Slowly there appeared a pulsing red and blue light about where my third eye is located. I felt surges of energy at my throat. I wasn't at all frightened by any of this because there is always a great deal of energy movement around the throat as the activation goes on.

The energy coming in through the mouth of God began to shift and move me into what the ancients call

"Samadhi," which is the deepest state of meditation. It is during that experience that you become unified with God. It is also a state where I usually lose contact with this reality and shift into awareness of higher dimensions, which is what happened.

After about ten minutes, the next thing I recall was Lorenzo suggesting I come back into this reality. During that period of Samadhi, I was aware of the boundaries between my physical self and the higher dimensions dissolving, but they quickly returned as I reentered this time and space. The incredible feeling you experience during that time you are one with the universe and God, goes far beyond words. I also felt the pulsing of the pineal gland in the center of my head. The pineal gland regulates the process of enlightenment in concert with the crown chakra, which emulates upward from the pineal through the top of the head.

As my third eye pulsed with that red and blue light I became aware of an awakening ability of my own to be able to see beyond time and space. As my ordinary experience of time and space melted away, the mystical self was being birthed as Lorenzo prayed and invoked the masters of ancient Egypt, Lemuria, and Atlantis. I was also aware of the great Hindu deities Shiva, Shakti, Nugatatwalla and others lending their energies to the experience. All the masters of the universe were present to celebrate my awakening into their mystical realm.

As the energy moved down along my spinal column and into my heart chakra, I could feel the release and cleansing of eons of karma around my heart center. The heart center is surrounded by what has been called the "veil of tears," and it is the last veil to be cleared on the path of enlightenment.

For days afterward I felt the cloak of the mystic about me as the higher aspects of my soul descended into my life.

One of the most fascinating aspects of the mouth of God is its connection with the transcendental dialogue. Those who speak with the angels and higher dimensions of God actually speak to them through the mouth of God. I can see that when people are channeling. The beings they are channeling actually enter their energies through the mouth of God. This activation is a must for all interested in enhancing their ability to communicate with God. The transcendental dialogue conveys far more than words. It contains feeling, knowing, understanding, wisdom, intuition, and insight. It is our connection to the higher levels of ourselves, which know everything.

About a week after arriving in Magdelina, I was sitting and thinking about my future. I wondered what I would do with what I was learning and how it might affect my life after I arrived home.

Just then a voice said, "What is it that you would like to do? What would make your heart sing?"

"Who is this?" I replied. "Who is speaking?"

"Does it matter?" the voice said.

"Well, no, but I would like some clarity. I have heard voices before but never so clearly."

"Who would you imagine it is?" The voice had a masculine quality to it. As an experienced channeler and medium, I had had many dialogues with beings from both the higher and lower realms. This voice seemed to speak with an authority that the others did not have. I thought to myself, I wonder if this is God speaking.

The voice immediately responded to my thought. "Do you really think you can hide your thoughts from me?"

The idea that the entity could easily read my thoughts was a little disconcerting to me. I asked point blank, "Is this God or is it my imagination?"

"Does it matter?" he replied. "Do you think that God cannot or would not come to you through your imagination?"

"Yes, I suppose he can, but I like to be clear on these matters."

"You are clear," he said, "but you constantly doubt that God speaks to you and guides your life. Take your own advice. Read your own words, those you have written in your new book. Did you think that just because you wrote your thoughts down in a book you would never forget them? Study your own words and thoughts on these matters until you cannot think any other thought but that of truth. You would doubt your own thoughts and ability to know truth. You all doubt your inner wisdom, but do you not know that your thought, your inner wisdom, are not really yours but God's? Where do you think these thoughts come from? Your culture, your society, your mass consciousness? Hardly. I want you and all who read your new book to know that your desires are my desires, your thoughts are my thoughts, your wisdom is my wisdom. I disperse it lovingly and constantly to you."

That voice still comes back to me from time to time, especially during those times when I temporarily forget his message.

The transcendental dialogue is certainly one of the most important aspects of connecting with the higher realms. I have become a much better channel since my own activation. The enhanced clarity helps me in many ways, including in my daily life. We see examples of transcendental dialogue when we work with psychics, channels, intuitives and masters. It is from those higher realms that what has been called "divine will" or "grace" actually comes. It is the conscious energy of the higher realms, and it contains humanity's evolutionary dialogue — the consciousness that we will all eventually become.

All the great inventions and advances of technology come from that realm and are the result of a direct, intuitive connection to the realm of the transcendental dialogue. Much of our current spiritual information has reached us through what we call channels. After all, don't we consider the Bible to be divinely inspired? In that process there is a connection to the higher realms. However, it is possible to be connected only to the astral plane and think one is connected to a much higher realm. There are also ways to be sure that doesn't happen. You must be very discerning when listening to channeled information because few channels are clear enough to deliver unbiased information; in fact, none are absolutely clear.

Yogananda is one of the most well-known and respected of the Indian gurus and masters who have come to us to teach and lecture. He is also the only one to address what he calls the mouth of God and explain its benefits.

An interesting fact about Yogananda is that even though he died decades ago, his body is still on display in California and has not decayed since the day of his death. In one of his books, he speaks of a woman who lived for fifty-nine years without drinking water or eating, but by breathing through the medulla.

Very little else has been written or known about the mouth of God until recently. There had also been no way to enhance its functioning in humans until the present day and age. Previously, you had to wait until you became enlightened or nearly enlightened before it became fully activated.

For those who have gained the status of enlightenment it becomes a vortex for transcendental higher level energies.

Many changes occur as a result of opening the mouth of God during and after the activation. Those higher-level frequencies flood the chakras and other energy systems with the consciousness-raising and growth-enhancing energies from the realm of Source. One of the most profound is a tremendous feeling or sense of expansion as you move beyond separation into unity consciousness.

The activation brought my higher self to the surface, which means that I began to see the world I live in through the wisdom of my higher self. This gave me a great sense of confidence in the decisions and choices I made from this perspective, because my higher self can, of course, see beyond time and space.

A shift to higher consciousness is hard to explain in worldly terms except that it contains increased wisdom and understanding of life itself, a greater awareness of expanded truth, more trust and faith in the universe, insight and awareness about your life and its purpose. I get stronger inner feelings and messages telling me what to do and when to do it, as well as warning signals when I am about to make a less favorable choice. On a day-to-day basis I simply make better choices.

After the activation I experienced a tremendous release of karma for about six months. Karma refers to issues that are stuck in your subconscious energies and often stem from other lifetimes. These issues are like magnets attracting negative experiences. Because karma is so subconscious, negative experiences result (and you don't know why), and you cannot do anything to prevent them. The influx of energy is so great with the mouth-of-God activation that much of my karma was simply moved out of my energy system, therefore negating many negative experiences in the future.

For some people the activation is so dynamic that it is truly a mind-blowing experience. The result of knowing and experiencing yourself as God is almost beyond comprehension. For others, there is a subtle yet unmistakable shift to higher consciousness, which may be known to them only in their dream states. Subtle or dynamic, a massive lifting and releasing of ancient and not-so-ancient karma occurs. In my own experience it felt as though there was just not enough room inside my head for whatever was going on. I awoke the next morning with a sense of being reborn into this world, with a constant awareness of my higher self/Christ consciousness having surfaced and shed the veil between my personality and my soul.

One woman who took the activation from me after I'd returned from New Mexico said that she didn't feel anything from the activation. But while accidentally rubbing her eyes with the palms of her hands afterwards, she said she could suddenly see the vastness of the higher dimensions, and all they contained — something she hadn't seen before.

Another man stated that he became so connected with God that he would forever walk the sacred path, which he discovered on the higher dimensions while taking the activation.

Scott Penman said that after experiencing the mouth of God himself, he felt considerably less weighed down by his body. More notably, the connection that the activation established with a larger part of his self has remained with him. Since undergoing the process, any time fear or worry raised their ugly heads in his mind, he hasn't fallen prey to their temptation. There was definitely a shift in his awareness, and the effects have been anything but subtle. He best described it by saying that as he goes through his day he feels the truth: "God is with us." After undergoing the activation, he feels as though space has opened inside of him that is still and silent — a quiet, light place where divinity dwells. Stranger still, he senses that all of his experience in that space thus far is only a beginning.

As the energy pours in through the mouth of God it can be a little disconcerting. I know it was for me. As the energy floods the chakras it cleans them, and removes the debris stored in those energy centers as those old programs surface and are released. Although this can be upsetting, it really is a shortcut. Ordinarily it could take years to access and become aware of all those issues and programs, whereas the energy entering the mouth of God may clear them in a few days or less.

When change occurs as a result of the activation you may begin to see the world and your life in a very different light. As said before, change can be hard for humans because ego finds change difficult if not abhorrent. Once the mouth of God is activated, change begins to occur — slowly for some, quickly for others, but change you will.

Polarity, of course, is the result of being focused in the world of the ego. But when that focus begins to change, you begin to shed polarity. No polarity exists at that point of entry we call the mouth of God. For some, there is a dramatic shift in the way they view their lives. In others, the shifts and changes are hardly noticed. But once the activation occurs, change becomes an inherent part of their lives.

Almost everyone's experience of the mouth of God is different. There are a few things that many experience as a result of the activation, and expansiveness is one of them. There is an actual change in the relationship between the electron and the atom: the space between them is increased. This creates a feeling of expansiveness and connection to God that is quite profound. There is a sense of becoming your higher nature. Along with this, there is a connection to the wisdom of that higher nature. Peace and tranquility are perhaps the most common states during and after the activation. People often become aware that they speak differently afterward, that there is a clarity to what they say that didn't exist before. The mouth of God is just above and behind the throat chakra and therefore closely connected to the mechanism of expression. Creativity will also be enhanced because self-expression is linked to the throat chakra.

As a facilitator, I can see what happens in people's energies as they take the initiation. The initiation is a three-step process. At each step the eighth chakra becomes brighter and brighter. It always amazes and impresses me when I see the eighth chakra take on more luminescent qualities. The eighth chakra also indicates how quickly people are transcending and leaving behind their old reality. The transition out of polarity into unity with God is identified in the eighth chakra.

My search for knowledge, information and understanding has taken me all over the world. I have studied with psychoanalysts, shamans and enlightened masters. The most esoteric teachings I have found are presented in a book by Pantanjali, an enlightened master who talks about the magic of the *Sidhis*. The *Sidhis* have been resurrected by the transcendental meditation movement, and are again taught, but to only the most advanced students. The *Sidhis* contain techniques for levitating, disappearing, bilocating and so on. The mouth of God technique was a lost *Sidhi* until it was given to Lorenzo by Simon Peter in a dream. It had been lost or misplaced for thousands of years and has been released to humanity now to help us with our spiritual growth and to release us from bondage to a polarized world. And if you're one of the millions who struggle every day, no doubt you, too, feel it couldn't have come at a better time.

But then again, of course it couldn't.

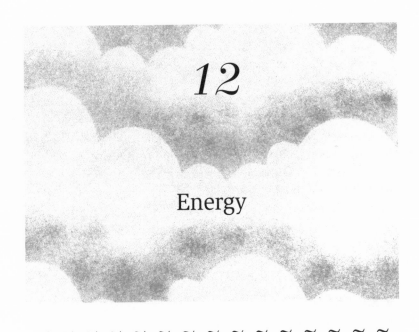

12

Energy

~ ~ ~ ~ ~ ~ ~ ~ ~ ~ ~ ~ ~ ~ ~

Ever since Einstein first proposed his theory of relativity with the formula $E=mc2$, we have come to see that everything is energy. We also now understand that energy cannot be destroyed. Changed and transformed, yes, but not destroyed. This includes you. You are energy and no part of you can be destroyed, which means that even death cannot destroy who you really are. Every enlightened teacher who has come to earth has taught that there is no death, only transition from one form to another. Nevertheless the fear of death is quite pervasive and underlies a great deal of stress in our culture. Ego fears death, believing its own annihilation is possible.

After all, don't we spend so much of our time trying to conquer the ego once and for all? Your soul, on the other hand, views death as transformation. Annihilation, of course, is impossible because energy cannot be destroyed.

The belief that death is the end of life is very much a western view. Most other cultures are aware of reincarnation and its ramifications. In Thailand, for example, the villagers will mark the body of the deceased so that when they are reborn they will remember who they were.

I recently witnessed a group of politicians grieving those who had died in Vietnam. The reason for their mourning was that those who had died could have become senators or congressmen after the war. It seemed to be an irreconcilable loss to them. But no doubt, the next generation of politicians will include those who had died in Vietnam. In fact, this may have already occurred. A friend of mine has a three-year-old son who was terrified of the aircraft that flew over their home. He actually talked about a time when he was big. We believe he was an older child in Vietnam who was killed by a bomb dropped from one of our planes.

Death is a core issue in the western world. We spend a great deal of time and energy trying to put off death and avoid the inevitable, because we think it is the end of life. This fear of death is at the root of much of your insecurity. It constantly undermines your sense of well-being. You will not be able to let go of your fear of death simply by reading about it. You will have to look within yourself to realize the truth of your immortality. As you do so, you'll begin to release one of the most troubling polarities — life versus death. There is really only life; there is no such thing as death.

Barbara came to me after her mother and father both had died in an auto accident. She had become so emotionally traumatized by their deaths that she was fixated on dying and felt an overwhelming fear of her own eventual death. She'd read many books that claimed there is no death, but she was raised in a religion that did not recognize an afterlife. She had become so focused on death and dying that it consumed her daily thoughts, to the point that she was unable to live normally.

I was able to regress her into experiencing her other lifetimes, and after several vivid regressions, she began to release her fear of death. She became so enthusiastic about her other lifetimes that we spent more time in them than was actually necessary. She realized that her fear of dying had originated in another lifetime which had ended in a torturous death. All areas of her life benefited from releasing this major fear of life itself.

Viewing energy in new ways can have several tremendous benefits, not the least of which are the benefits to your everyday living.

Ron had spent many years in therapeutic processes and modalities and he had certain issues that, although he was fully aware of them, kept reappearing. He was desperately seeking a way to completely release those old patterns when he came to see me. As all patterns are energetic, I explained to him that we could clear the issues using transformative energy techniques. He had a lifelong pattern of anger about his mother's untimely death, and even though he was aware of it and had worked through many of his feelings surrounding her, he still struggled with his anger. I suggested that we use a symbolic approach. I asked him to imagine that he was holding his anger in his hands. I asked him to add light to it. Then, together we recited an ancient mantra designed to intensify the experience. Suddenly he experienced an explosion in his hands and he felt the old pattern lift and fade from sight. He proclaimed that he was done with the anger, and to this day, many years later, the issue has not arisen again.

You are a complex system of conscious energy frequencies. Not only is it physically impossible to destroy energy, but all transformation occurs energetically. It is the real level at which we are all transforming. The physical body is atomic, electronic energy, and it evolves by taking on energies that actually increase the spin of the electrons. The increase in the speed of electrons causes a decrease in the density of your body, bringing the body closer to its energetic state, the state of pure consciousness. This is the process of ascension, the climb to a consciousness that is uncluttered by the slower, denser energies of fear.

Your emotional and mental bodies are also electronic, but non-atomic. Atomic energy has mass, weight and size; it takes up space. Non-atomic energy doesn't have those qualities. There is a non-atomic, etheric body that holds the template for the physical body. Psychics often see it as a blue haze that extends several inches beyond the physical body. Any change in your physical body actually occurs first at the etheric level.

As your consciousness grows, you raise the frequencies of your energy bodies. Any emotional clearing work you do allows higher frequencies to come into the physical body and its energy systems. That is also what is accomplished during meditation. The altered state of meditation creates a pathway to higher energies. Raising the frequency of your consciousness is the real work of spiritual transformation. You are conscious energy, and you can grow in consciousness by taking in higher energy frequencies. You can completely transform your reality by consciously taking on higher frequencies. There are any number of techniques for doing just that, which are discussed at length in my other books, *Ancient Wisdom* and *Creating Your Light Body*.

The organs of your energy systems are your chakras. You have twelve major chakras, seven within the body and five without. Each of these two chakra systems represents a different range of frequencies. The chakras outside the body are of a much higher, finer frequency than the others. Your soul energy is represented by the eighth chakra, which is about six inches above your head. The first major evolutionary step you can take actually anchors the eighth chakra within the physical body. Prior to that happening, there is very little of your soul's consciousness within your physical consciousness. Higher energies, such as the consciousness of your soul, are more intelligent, more compassionate and more loving. Taking on those energies will help you develop these qualities in yourself. It will also increase your intuition, creativity, and inner knowing.

As with any skill, there are some who have a natural ability to take on higher energies, but most do not. The most adept handlers of the higher energies are the beings who reside in other realms, to whom we refer as angels and guides, and living masters who reside on Earth. Through practice, interest and a natural aptitude, I have developed the ability to transmit higher energies to others. I also teach people how to integrate those higher energies into their own energy systems. As you raise the frequencies of your physical, emotional and mental bodies, you actually begin to shed the habitual thinking patterns that have blindly dictated your thought processes for so long.

Because we are such mental beings, many people may think that working with and being sensitive to subtle energies is confusing and esoteric. It isn't something our scientific community or our schools teach, but this doesn't mean it isn't a very real thing. There are several energy modalities being used today, hands-on disciplines such as

Reiki, Shen, Cranial Sacral, and so on. There are classes for beginner, intermediate, and advanced energy workers. It is important to note that because you are conscious energy, it is natural for you to work with and command those energies.

Those who wish to evolve and grow spiritually need to learn how to work with their energies. Attend basic chakra alignment and hands-on healing classes, or any others that will help you begin to understand your own energetic nature. You'll be amazed at the ease with which you can harmonize your own energies or the energies of another, as well as the environment you live in.

Stress is so much a part of modern life that without being able to compensate for it in some fashion you will be at a great disadvantage. No one is exempt from the constant disruption in the harmonic flow of the planet's energy systems. This means you will have to make an effort to harmonize your energies in order to change the way your life looks. You feel stress as the result of your energy bodies being out of alignment with each other. You must find peace in that place where your consciousness is now — your body. You can release your stress and harmonize your energy bodies in a matter of minutes once the technique is learned.

Deep breathing is an excellent tool for realigning your energies. There are quite a few modalities that use breathing to harmonize your emotional body, but westerners are by nature notoriously shallow breathers. When a threat is perceived, either emotionally or physically, you will almost always hold your breath, and contract your energies. Doing so throws your energy bodies out of harmony and alignment, creating stress and dysfunction in all of your energy systems, including your mental body. When a threat exists in your mind (which is the only place a constant threat *can* exist) you begin to suppress your breathing. Your breathing reflects the state of your mind and bodies, and vice versa. Becoming mindful of your breathing can literally work wonders toward transforming fear.

By consciously making an effort toward harmonizing your energies, you will take in higher frequencies of energy, increasing your level of consciousness and awareness. Of course all of us, whether consciously or unconsciously, find ourselves in the perfect flow of energy from time to time. Athletes call this "the zone." They speak the language of body chemistry and hormones, but whether they know it or not, the zone begins at an atomic and energetic level. Sometimes it occurs while meditating, walking on the beach, exercising, or just sitting and listening to soothing music.

Your energies seek harmony. The natural state of existence is balanced. Because harmony is so often disrupted you become habitually out of balance. Any contraction or stressful state is unnatural and will decrease your ability to survive and resolve the problems in your life. Here on Earth we experience alternating currents, negative to positive, so it is difficult to remain detached from the negative aspect. If everyone's energies were completely harmonized, within a very short time all fear would cease to exist. Life would be balanced, harmonious, and blissful.

Love is energy. It is the highest frequency, the backdrop of energy that supports all others. Your ability to connect with the higher energies enhances your ability to experience love, the most healing frequency of all. And of course love is the polar opposite of fear. How simple it really is, yet how difficult we have made it. People who experience the pure frequencies of love immediately begin to transform all negative polarities to positives and move to a higher state of consciousness, wisdom and clarity.

Often the energies we experience are quite negative, and are low, slow vibrations. Because of the law of resonance, you tend to easily get stuck in the lower energies of the earth plane. But of course there is also a natural attraction to the higher frequencies of love — yet another example of the dichotomy created by polarity. If you are consistent in your efforts to bring in the higher energies available to you, there will be a permanent shift in your own energetic structure. Similarly, there will be a shift in your consciousness. You'll be less attracted to the lower vibrations and frequencies of fear, and more connected to the higher vibrations and frequencies of love. In this period of constant change and flux in which we live today, when the energies of the planet are constantly moving to a higher vibration, survival requires a propensity for adaptation. You may never have thought of it that way, but like all species, man's survival as a group and as individuals requires great skills of adaptation.

You have natural abilities to sense and work with energy. God did not create hopeless, helpless beings. God created beings of enormous capabilities, of heroic deeds in everyday life. Influencing your own energy systems is by no means out of the question. People do it every day when they take multi-vitamins. Anything ingested to change the way you feel affects your energies first. There is no reason you cannot have a strong influence over the energies that affect your consciousness. You can raise them to higher states, and as you do so, remove the major reason for poor health. All disease is a symbolic response to fear; fear is the basis for everything that goes wrong emotionally and phys-ically, yet it is simply energy and subject to natural physical laws and natural spiritual laws. It is energy that can be changed and transformed. This is the basis of miraculous healing.

The benefits of working with energy are great when you begin to connect with the frequencies of your higher nature and purge the energy of fear. You begin to reestablish your connection not only to your own higher consciousness, but to the natural order of the universe, and all the wisdom and intelligence therein. Higher consciousness is attained by bringing higher frequencies of energy into your own energies and anchoring them there. As you do so, you begin to dispel and transform your lower energies. Actually, you're doing this in a modest way whenever you create awareness of, and release, old issues or traumas. I say modest, because when you learn to work directly with higher energies, you can greatly speed and enhance the results, and grow and evolve much faster. Raising the frequency of your energetic bodies is not just a parlor game. It is the serious business of growth and change. It is, in truth, conscious evolution. If you did nothing else but work on clearing your energy fields, you would greatly enhance your ability to survive this lifetime. Doing so will naturally gravitate you toward higher and higher energy sources, toward love, and toward God.

13

Commitment

~ ~ ~ ~ ~ ~ ~ ~ ~ ~ ~ ~ ~ ~ ~ ~

The challenges we all face when making changes in the way we think and the beliefs we base our lives upon are no doubt well known to the reader by now. Foremost are the polarities that exist in this relative world in which we all reside. Neither you nor anyone else can escape the dynamic shifting from negative to positive that holds this plane of existence together. The constant vigil required to stay in the neutral zone isn't easy. It will demand your conscious effort. Of course your ego would rather just go on automatic pilot, hoping that something out there will change. And it might, eventually. You might suddenly somehow find yourself on the positive side of polarity, not even knowing how you got there. True to this method of dealing with reality, you may just as likely find yourself unexpectedly back on the negative end of experience.

Your assignment — should you choose to accept it — is to stay balanced between polarities. This neutral zone is the most agreeable state to be in, as well as the most natural state. It is the place where all experiences are both positive and negative at the same time, and therefore neutral and not in need of judgment. Eventually, everyone will master the art of integrating polarities. When that happens, a new way of life will begin in this universe. It is in this place of neutral observation that God can speak to you, and all things come together with ease. It is the center of the river, where the currents of life meet the least resistance.

Judgment is the great destabilizer in a polar world where everything is endlessly categorized as either good or bad. How easily we dictate that some things are unacceptable and certainly not a part of a divine plan. The truth is that you cannot find peace in a universe you cannot accept. Becoming non-judgmental is perhaps the most difficult of all the things you must do to change your life. Rarely do you think to yourself, "This is the way it is, and I needn't judge anything here." Yet this is the only stance that will lead you to higher ground. Anything else simply leads to more experiences of polarization, because your judgments all turn inward and create dissonance within your own energies. Through resonance, this sets up the process of attracting that which you judge. As the natural order of the universe seeks harmony and balance within the singular energy system of "all that is," your disharmony will be met with a reflection of equal disharmony. You could declare that everything is wonderful all the time, but denial never creates harmony, and that part of you that knows this will tag your attempt at self deception as nothing but BS. It is not enough to say that you believe: You must trust.

This book is a call to action to all of those who would embrace the mythical spiritual warrior. It is for those who choose to commit their lives to change. In order to do that you must go within. You must discover clarity and learn to listen to the voice of wisdom that has been deemed an inner quality. The voice of wisdom comes out of the neutral zone. It is neither inner nor outer, it simply is. Contemplation and meditation are the tools we use to evoke the universal wisdom of the divine intelligence, from wherever it may come.

Your choices, for the most part, are motivated from deep within your psyche, and are simply feeding your psychological needs and desires. For however long you have lived, you have been acting out of a program that you learned very early in life from your family, friends and society. Ego projects the past forward in an attempt to continually validate those programs that have become your reality. Your ego could care less whether or not those old tapes and programs are in alignment with universal principles. Your life is a replica of your inner, psychological terrain. Your beliefs have been the map leading you to where you are today. As long as the landscape is shaped with a fearful ego, this world will reflect your disharmony. The process of change is one that begins in what we have called your inner world. It starts with you and your thinking.

The neutral zone is that place of wisdom, clarity, and knowing which everyone possesses. It is truly neither inner nor outer. That state of mind is most easily accessed while meditating, or during periods of great contemplation. Meditation allows you to shed the skin of the reality in which you are currently ensconced. When you meditate, you loosen the bonds of the material world.

While meditation alone will not accomplish everything you desire, it is an integral part of the process of evolution and change. There are as many forms of meditation as there are people who meditate. In fact, today there is a renaissance of many of the ancient techniques that have been used for centuries in the Far East. As you begin to spend more time in the neutral zone, you'll be led to whichever methods and techniques are appropriate for you. Personally, one of the most effective forms of meditation I have experienced is Bija meditation; which I now teach. Meditation is a key ingredient to the process of surviving and reinventing your life into what you want it to be. Whatever your choice of meditation styles, the more you meditate, the more easily you will be able to inhabit the neutral zone.

No one has risen to higher states of consciousness who hasn't spent considerable time in altered states of consciousness. Meditation is an act of altering your state of consciousness. The moment you reduce the speed or frequency of your brain waves, you can clearly hear the wisdom of your higher consciousness.

Everyone resists change to one degree or another. It is the courage to walk faithfully through the doorway of change into the land of the unknown that separates the warriors from the wimps. You can wimp out on your life if you want, because no one is looking. You may get some flack from your mate, your children, or some author, but what do they know? Now that you have read one more book what are you going to do? Go on to the next one hoping that some of what you have read will stick? Or are you going to commit to change? If you desire change, then you must integrate into your psyche and energies a new road map for your way of being.

For the generations that have passed, it was unheard of to make a great deal of change in the way they conducted their lives. For a few there was psychoanalysis as per Freudian schooling, and that was about it. An expanded knowledge and understanding of the human psyche has come from colleges and universities within the last half-century. During the sixties and seventies forms of self-discovery began to emerge, although for the most part these modalities have remained quite academic in their approach to people. Still, there is a place for all of these therapies. My own daughter is seeing a psychoanalyst at my recommendation, because I felt that at this time in her life she would benefit most from classical, analytical therapy for depression. She benefited from antidepressants, recovered quickly, and no longer uses them.

Most of you will want a quicker, more formidable system than psychoanalysis with which you can begin to change your life. The first stage is simply to let go of control and begin to trust in the universe. The ease with which you are able to do this may depend upon whether this is your first exposure to this concept of surrender, or one in a string of many. Breaking the hold that your ego's need to control has on you is a major step. Most of us are highly trained and experienced experts at the art of control. Letting go is dependent upon your willingness to try something different. Such willingness usually comes out of the realization that what you've been doing thus far simply isn't working. Unfortunately, many people have to hit bottom before they decide to change. I hope you will decide to let go of control somewhere between the time you recognize the need for change and the time you hit bottom.

The decision to trust in the support and generosity of the universe may be the result of having tried something else for several lifetimes, then coming into a lifetime where the option to trust in God becomes the only way for you to move ahead with your own evolution and change. Your inability to know what has happened in your other lifetimes doesn't negate those past experiences. They are very influential in a way that is hard to convey if you are convinced this lifetime is where and who you are. One single thread may weave its way through lifetime after lifetime. You have a unique opportunity now to break any threads that impede your growth, to step outside of the habitual experiences of this lifetime or any other, and make dramatic changes with ease. When you step out of control and begin to trust, you immediately enter the neutral zone where all things can happen, and can happen quickly and easily.

Faith is the catalyst for all growth and change. It is faith that truly moves mountains and creates an opening for change. Faith requires action. You have to move energy to accomplish your goals. You must act to seal your faith. The trick is to choose goals that are in alignment with universal principles and your soul's purpose. Those inspirations that come to you from the quiet and stillness of the neutral zone (during meditation, contemplation, prayer, or even just walking) are the ones that will move you to the highest ground in the quickest manner.

We have discussed personal will before, but it is worth mentioning again because it can become such an impediment to the natural order of life. Your personal will comes out of your lower chakras, predominantly your third chakra. Personal will is the domain of ego and personality, and it is what has guided you to where you are now. Stop and think about this. Your ego is likely going ape at the thought of giving up its cherished position as captain of your ship, but allowing yourself to be constantly guided by your personal will is tantamount to rearranging the deck chairs on the Titanic.

Your history in this lifetime and all others has been played out by the various personalities you have had over those many lifetimes. If you can find one, including this one, in which following the dictates of ego and personal will has lead you to higher ground and a life of ease and bliss, you are doing better than I am. But if you're like the rest of us, and allow yourself to be led by the ego, you will always be projecting the past forward and reliving those old programs you learned in early childhood.

Giving up your personal will really is not giving up anything at all. Humans were created to live a life guided by the higher realms. Somewhere along the way you were seduced by the illusion of power, greed, control, and the possibility that you could shed responsibility for your own actions. Over time, you fell from grace. Living in the neutral zone is the return of your life into a state of grace.

Outside of the zone, along the edges of the river of life, there are many things that catch your attention: sexuality, influence, power, material possessions, all of which are promised by your ego to make you feel better about yourself. But these are the illusions of a material world. Rarely do such benefits ease the pain in your life. In fact, once you finally do acquire them and they do not ease the pain, there is even greater stress and anxiety because you believed the lie and now do not know where to turn.

The only place you can turn for refuge is to the neutral zone. In that quietude you will find the grace of God showing you the way of rebirth.

Those of you who have been walking this path for a long time probably have heard much of the information that comes through channels and psychics about the changes taking place on Earth at this time. The Earth is partaking of a shift into higher frequencies of energy, and special dispensation has been given to the inhabitants of Earth for unparalleled growth and change. You have a unique opportunity now that was not even available to you before May of 1996, to move beyond those old programs that are the result of cause and effect, and live from the neutral zone without interference from those old and often ancient historical programs of your karma.

What you have just read is the simplest truth, and the easiest route you can follow to lead you from where you are in life to where you want to be. Your own commitment, combined with faith and action, is the tool of transformation and survival. No one is incapable of change, yet few people believe they can take their destiny into their own hands. It takes trust to move mountains. Your commitment to your life is entirely your concern. It could even be that this lifetime is perfect just the way it is, even if it doesn't seem to be working well. Only you can determine if this is true for you. All you have to do is listen to that still, small voice within.

You will go on to read other books, many of which will probably speak of great esoteric teachings and systems that promise accelerated evolution and change. Some of them will actually deliver on that promise, and some will not. You may even find a guru, or maybe you will become your own teacher. Once you have shifted into a higher state of consciousness and find yourself on a new plateau, you will need to get back to the basics because they are what allowed you to make the shift in the first place. Every time you create a shift you will need to get back to the basics. You will discover that truth is relative, and each time you read this information you will gain something and see it in a different light. When that occurs, perhaps you will pull this book from the shelf and read it again. The authors have traveled this path for many years, and still find it necessary to periodically get back to the basics. After all, even visionary writers use the very elementary alphabet.

About the Author

Richard Dupuis is the author of two books, *Creating Your Light Body* and *Ancient Wisdom*.

Richard has been studying and writing about metaphysical principles and information for more than twenty years. He has traveled and taught classes on metaphysical subjects and the Ascension process throughout the United States. As a student of many of the Ascended Masters, Richard has studied both the ancient and modern teachings of the perennial wisdom. He is well known for his ability as a channel and psychic.

Richard is one of the pioneers in developing new techniques to help people release their past and begin their journey to enlightenment. He has helped numerous people to improve their lives through his counseling and by applying his meditation techniques to increase their awareness of Soul and Spirit. He is an ordained minister of the Council of Light and lives in Seattle, Washington.

~ ~ ~ ~ ~

TO CONTACT RICHARD DUPUIS ABOUT SPONSORING A WORKSHOP IN YOUR AREA, A MOUTH-OF-GOD ACTIVATION, FREE NEWSLETTER SERVICE, COUNSELING, BOOKS AND TAPES CALL:

1-800-480-6021

Order Form for Books and Tapes
by Richard Dupuis

TAPES		PRICE		QTY	AMOUNT
		U.S.	CANADA		
1.	Activating Your Soul Star	$9.95	$12.95		
2.	The Ascension Series	29.95	38.95		
3.	Beginning Your Journey to Mastery	29.95	38.95		
4.	Creating Your Light Body	59.95	77.95		
5.	The Vibrational Energy Centers	59.95	77.95		
	BOOKS				
1.	Ancient Wisdom	10.95	13.95		
2.	Creating Your Light Body	9.95	11.95		
			SUB TOTAL		
			*SHIPPING & HANDLING		
			TOTAL		

Shipping and Handling Charges

Orders up to $15.00	$2.50	$35.01 to $50.00	$6.25
$15.01 to $25.00	$3.50	$50.01 to $75.00	$8.00
$25.01 to $35.00	$4.00	$75.01 & over	$9.75

SHIP TO: NAME

STREET ADDRESS

CITY STATE ZIP

YOUR PHONE NUMBER HOME PHONE WORK PHONE
(in case we need to call
you about your order)

Make checks payable to: Richard Dupuis
4742 42nd Avenue S.W. #608
Seattle, WA 98116
Telephone: 1-800-480-6021

To order additional copies of

From the Mouth of God

Book: $14.95   Shipping/Handling $3.50

Contact: **BookPartners, Inc.**
P.O. Box 922, Wilsonville, OR 97070
Fax: 503-682-8684
Phone 503-682-9821
Phone: 1-800-895-7323